Secret Laws of Attraction

The Effortless Way to Get the Relationship You Want

Talane Miedaner

AUTHOR OF THE INTERNATIONAL BESTSELLER
Coach Yourself to Success

Mc Graw Hill

New York   Chicago   San Francisco   Lisbon   London   Madrid   Mexico City
Milan   New Delhi   San Juan   Seoul   Singapore   Sydney   Toronto

Library of Congress Cataloging-in-Publication Data

Miedaner, Talane.
    The secret laws of attraction : the effortless way to get the relationship you want /
Talane Miedaner.
        p.   cm.
    Includes index.
    ISBN-13: 978-0-07-154375-0 (alk. paper)
    ISBN-10: 0-07-154375-9 (alk. paper)
   1. Mate selection   2. Man-woman relationships.   3. Self-consciousness
(Awareness)   4. Communication.   I. Title.

HQ801.M559   2008
646.7'7—dc22   2007046459

1 2 3 4 5 6 7 8 9 10 11 12 13 14 15 16 17 18 19 20 21 FGR/FGR 0 9 8

ISBN 978-0-07-154375-0
MHID   0-07-154375-9

Interior design by Monica Baziuk

McGraw-Hill books are available at special quantity discounts to use as premiums and sales promotions or for use in corporate training programs. To contact a representative, please visit the Contact Us pages at www.mhprofessional.com

The instructions and advice in this book are not intended as a substitute for therapy or psychological counseling. The author and publisher disclaim any responsibility or liability resulting from actions advocated or discussed in this book. In the interest of preserving client confidentiality, all client names, and, in some cases, identifying characteristics have been changed. The scenarios, situations, and results are real.

This book is printed on acid-free paper.

CONTENTS

· · · · · · · · ·

ACKNOWLEDGMENTS

. . . .

MY DEEPEST GRATITUDE and profound thanks to:

My incredible mother, Penelope, who volunteered to come and look after six-month-old Sophia for four months so that I could get some sleep and be cogent enough to write this book. I could never have done it without your support as I was completely and utterly exhausted. Not only did you do the night feeds, which would have been more than enough, but you cooked countless meals, designed our new loft space, dug out the garden, and looked after Kaela as well. In your spare time you even managed to read and edit the manuscript! I am eternally grateful and cannot thank you enough for all your love, encouragement, and support. I count my lucky stars that you are my mother!

Johanna Bowman, my fabulous editor, for your enthusiasm, your insightful comments, and your careful and thoughtful editing. You've put your heart and soul into this book, not to mention loads of time and energy. Fiona Sarne, for your great suggestions. Charlie Fisher and his production team for their excellent copyediting, and a huge thank-you to the design and publicity team, especially Ann Pryor, Heather Cooper, and Sally Ashworth, at McGraw-Hill for such professional, quality work. And of course, a very special thanks to my publisher, Judith McCarthy, for seeing the potential in this book and making sure it got into the right hands.

My agent, Bonnie Solow, for encouraging me to go on my own with this book and for your continued support and guidance. You are very generous.

Winnie Shows, for your help in getting the book proposal written and your editorial assistance, in addition to your enthusiastic support of these ideas.

The extraordinary team at Talane Coaching Company who contributed their ideas to this book and to the Emotional Index Quiz: Judy Lowry, Eddie Marmol, Kathee Hill, Monica Howden, Sue Seel, and Terry O'Neill. You are not only wonderful human beings but also great coaches. Thank you for your ongoing love, support, and contribution. And a very special thanks to Faye Morgan, my marvellous assistant, for your positive support and superb organization over all these years. You've kept the business going through thick and thin and continue as cheerful as ever.

Amy Boucher Pye, for being a truly supportive friend and editor as well. I appreciate your efforts in presenting the book overseas and your excellent advice and suggestions, not to mention supplying me with brownies and pumpkin pie in England!

Vic Bosiger, for your tremendous work with the audio programs and the radio publicity, not to mention your enthusiastic support of my coaching in general. You are a remarkable human being, and I am blessed to have you in my life.

My dearest friends—Tracey, John, Kate, Dave, Allegra, Erik, Sam, Tony, Rachel, Sally, Debbie, and Colin—for your love, friendship, and ongoing support of my writing and coaching. Thank you for being completely understanding when I've been holed up writing and you don't hear from me for ages.

My sisters, Sarelyn and Keralee, for always being there for me. I love you and am so grateful to have you in my life.

My father, Terrel, for passing on your writing gene. Who'd have thought I'd get it? I appreciate your long-distance support and encouragement and for reminding me to hide out in order to get the work done.

Nancy Davidson, thank you for your wonderful insights and support in my life. Without you, I might not have recognized my husband for the great man he is. I am very grateful!

David Roth-Ey, for your continued friendship and enthusiastic support. You've been urging me to write this book for years.

The late Thomas Leonard, the founder of Coach U—I'm not the only coach who misses you and the brilliant spark that you created in this world. And I must acknowledge the late Abraham Maslow, whose early work on emotional needs and values forms the backbone of this book.

Sandy Vilas, the owner of Coach Inc., for your continued support and encouragement and your inspired leadership and coaching. You never cease to amaze me.

My first coach, Thom Politico, who first introduced me to coaching. I am ever grateful for all your coaching and support. You turned my life around and helped me find my true calling.

All the men I've ever dated, I enjoyed it all immensely and am grateful to each of you for the wonderful experiences and times we shared together. I needed to learn a lot about love and I thank you for the opportunity.

All my clients, for sharing their deepest and very personal emotional needs and values with me. I am grateful to have had the opportunity to be a part of your lives and hope that your stories become the inspiration for countless others. Thank you for being so courageous, open, and generous.

All my readers around the world who have sent so many wonderful e-mails about the great results you've achieved in your lives. It is my honor and privilege to have had such a positive impact. Thank you for asking me when the next book is coming out. It keeps me going to know you want more.

And last, but not least, my wonderful husband, Paul. Thank you for your unflagging belief in me and your tremendous love and support. You have given me the greatest gifts in life—love, laughter, companionship, and best of all, our two beautiful girls.

INTRODUCTION

· · · · · · · ·

Thirty-Seven and Still Single

As a life coach, I've discovered that most people want pretty much the same stuff: they want to have a career or work that is fulfilling and satisfying; they want to have money for the security and fun it can provide; and last but certainly not least, they want to have a loving relationship. Some people also want to add kids to that mix, but for most folks, this is the basic formula for happiness in life.

This book deals specifically with the love part and is written for those who are either looking for the love of their life or are in a relationship but, for some reason or another, still don't feel satisfied.

So what qualifies me to write this book? I've coached thousands of people to success in all areas of their life—including finding the right relationship and reaching career and personal goals. As the owner and founder of Lifecoach.com, I have years of experience giving advice online as well as by phone to people all over the world. I've been a senior trainer at Coach U where I received my training and certification as a Master Coach, and I lead seminars and workshops internationally on effortlessly attracting love, people, and success. However, perhaps more important than any specific coaching credentials is my personal experience of finding the man of my dreams.

Several years ago I was a successful professional in New York City, a fun-loving blonde who never had too much trouble finding a date. I always thought that I would keep dating and meeting men until one day I'd find just the right one, fall madly in love, and we'd marry and live happily ever after. In the meantime, I followed what I thought to be the correct dating strategy—I'd date three or four men (but not go to bed with any of them), then of that bunch, end up going out with one of them and develop an intimate, long-term relationship ranging from six months to four years. When I thought the relationship had no future potential I'd break up with him and start the process over again.

Now, I could very easily paint a fairly impressive picture of myself. I could legitimately say that I've dated about fifty interesting men from various regions of the world and had four marriage proposals from some very wealthy and intelligent men, all of which I turned down before finding the love of my life. While this is true, the full truth isn't nearly as glamorous and actually doesn't make me look very good at all. The real story is that although I was very successful and confident on one level, I was much needier than I realized. I kept attracting the wrong men in my life and didn't realize I would keep doing so until I sorted out my deepest personal and emotional needs. And that wasn't easy. If you'd like to learn the gory details, read on.

While pursuing my master's in English at Georgetown University in Washington, D.C., in my early twenties, I met a man who was thirty-five. We fell passionately in love. After a month of seeing each other constantly, we were engaged and I was over the moon with joy. This was it! I couldn't believe that even going to the grocery store with him could be so exciting. The chemistry was positively sizzling. I couldn't get enough of him and he couldn't get enough of me. We were head over heels in love.

Then we had an argument and he broke off the engagement. I was devastated. The next day he came back on bended knee pleading with me to take him back—he had made a terrible mistake. I took him back. Then a month later we had a fight and he literally ripped the ring off my finger and stormed out. The next day he was back again, begging forgiveness. We were engaged and disengaged six times in one summer—the most intense, passionate, emotional roller-coaster ride of my life. It got so that my best girlfriend forewarned her guests at a brunch to look at my hand for the ring before saying anything, because she was never sure if I was currently engaged or not.

I was so distraught and emotionally drained that I booked an appointment with a therapist. After one very teary hour, the man dispassionately said, "You don't have to marry this man." Strangely enough, this one statement set me free and gave me permission to end the relationship once and for all. I gave him back the ring and told him that this time there was no coming back; I could never marry him. He was persistent: he wrote letters; he sent flowers, cards, gifts; he called. But I stayed firm and hung up on him time and time again. Eventually he gave up.

This was my first experience of passion and I was lucky to have had it early on as I realized that pure passion, as exciting as it is, is not the best ingredient for a loving, stable relationship. I knew that I could never have kids with this man because I couldn't trust that he would be there.

A few years later I dated the most generous man I have ever known who was well liked by my friends and family. In fact, it was a girlfriend who first introduced us. We had a great two years together and then it came time to take the relationship to the next level. He was on the verge of asking me to marry him, so I decided we had better talk about our faiths. He was an Israeli Jew and, although not particularly religious, wanted me to convert to Judaism and raise our children in the Jewish faith. I said no. I could respect his beliefs, but I wasn't going to convert. A part of me knew this would be a problem all along, but I waited two years before I brought up the topic. This ended my relationship with my Jewish boyfriend, and we were both heartbroken and couldn't see each other without bursting into tears.

I started seeing a French man who enticed me with promises of travel and adventure. So off I went to Paris for excitement and adventure with my chic Frenchman. But after a few trips back and forth, this relationship ended with him owing me a couple hundred dollars (which, to his credit, he repaid a few years later). The relationship fizzled out after that and I was out there dating again. Around the same time, a foreign client at the bank offered me ten thousand dollars if I would marry him for a green card. I declined this offer as well. My third proposal, albeit a fraudulent one!

Then I met a fellow at a party and we started going out. I was immediately attracted, not by his looks, but by his chutzpah—a Yiddish word which sounds like what it is—breathtaking, unabashed boldness. On our first date he invited me to the Radio City Christmas Show with the Rockettes. He met me at the bank and we thought we'd see the latest art exhibit at the Museum of Modern Art on the way over. To our dismay, there were lines around the block. I suggested we skip it, but he was not so easily put off. To this day, I do not know how he managed to convince the girl at the counter to give us two tickets for free and let us in ahead of this huge queue of people. We had the whole place to ourselves. I was very impressed.

Then we went to get a bite to eat, but every bar and restaurant had an hour or more wait, which would make us late for the show. He thought of another plan and pulled me through the crowds and into a swanky hotel where there was a big office holiday party. He walked right up to the table and, after studying the name tags, complained that his wasn't there. The young lady apologized and quickly wrote up a tag for him. Then he said I was his guest, so she wrote up a name tag for me as well, and before I knew what was happening, we were in. The most incredible array of hors d'oeuvres, wines, champagne, and roasts lay before us. We ate to our heart's content, made small talk with a few people, then dashed off to the show where, compliments of his brother-in-law, we had front-row seats. An incredible evening to say the least. I should have realized right then that we had very different levels of integrity, not to mention different faiths that would rule out the prospect for marriage, but I was having such a good time I ended up dating him for more than six months. It wasn't until his shenanigans finally caught up with him and he got fired from his job that I realized this relationship wasn't right for me and we broke up.

I didn't understand that my unmet needs were driving me to the wrong men. But the most difficult thing for me to admit is that I even started dating a married man who was recently separated from his wife. I knew that I had no business going out with him, as he wouldn't be legally available for two years, but for some reason (my unmet needs), I still did. My own lack of integrity was revealed. We ended up going out for four years before I finally broke it off when I sensed he was getting ready to propose. By that time, he was legally divorced and we could have gotten married—my fourth proposal—but I never really wanted to marry him from the beginning. I just enjoyed going out with him.

So after going merrily along as a happy-go-lucky singleton in her twenties, here I was, all of the sudden, thirty-seven years old, still single, and with no real marital prospects in sight. I finally was in a place to ask, what happened?

When I look back at the history of my relationships, it reveals something very telling—my unconscious driving needs. I had a history of going out with men who on the one hand cherished me, but whom I never really intended to marry because of religious differences or because they were already married or emotionally unavailable. This very handily fulfilled two of my core needs: to be cherished and to be independent.

It was only when I did some work on my personal needs that I realized how much these unmet core needs were driving me in relationships. It explained why I was attracting and attracted to the wrong men. I would get wined and dined and cherished, but at the same time I could keep my independence. I wasn't consciously doing this because I wasn't even aware of what my needs were until I started doing the coaching work. And needs are so powerful they will drive you to do the darndest things, things that you *know* you shouldn't do, but can't help doing (such as overeating, going out with married men, or even spending too much).

Having delved into my needs, I had to face the fact that when I fell madly in love with someone, it was probably for all the wrong reasons. It was hard for me to believe that this Hollywood feeling of pure bliss was a really a big red flag for the *wrong man*! OK, so now I was armed with a very important piece of information: just because I'm not head over heels doesn't mean that there is no prospect for a happy and fulfilling marriage. In fact, when I do fall head over heels in "love," I should run in the opposite direction. The men I fell passionately in love with were all wrong for me, although I had been completely blind to it at the time. (This is what they are talking about when they say love is blind.) No one could have convinced me otherwise, I was so certain it was right with every cell and fiber of my body and soul because my needs were being met and it felt wonderful!

After my revelation, I went to work on deliberately and consciously fulfilling my top needs in healthy ways and telling my dearest friends and family exactly what I needed from them. A number of benefits ensued: (1) I noticed that I started attracting a different caliber of people in my life; (2) I had more money so I didn't *need* a man with riches (and then attracted a wealthy man!); (3) I was increasingly confident in all areas of my life; and (4) I raised my standards and didn't go out with married men nor did I put up with bad behavior from anyone. And, best of all, I no longer needed a man to enable me to live the life I'd always dreamed of. I was now truly ready to attract someone who shared the same values and goals.

It is now clear to me that if I hadn't done this work, I would not have attracted the incredible man that my husband is. He would have found me too needy. In this book, I've shared the tools you'll need to identify your top four emotional and personal needs and exactly what to do to fulfill them so that they don't drive you into the wrong relationships. And, if you are already in a relationship, you'll discover that meeting your own needs rekindles the love that may be dwindling.

About the time I began my inner work, I started dating a very nice Englishman I met while in London doing something I am incredibly passionate about—giving a coaching skills seminar. The relationship was so effortless, it was, well, almost boring. He was as comfortable as an old shoe and being with him was rather like breathing; you don't notice it until you stop. And it sounds horrible to say, but I thought he couldn't be The One *because* it was so easy, and he didn't fit my picture of the perfect man (I had secretly imagined I'd marry a tall, dark, broad-shouldered, Clark Kent sort of fellow—yes, Superman!). With Paul, there were no dramas whatsoever. We just had a great time together, loved traveling to foreign countries, and could talk about anything and everything—a real soul mate.

When he proposed, I was thrilled. And there you have it. Once I did the hard work of exploring my core needs and getting them met I was finally in a position to attract the right man. And, when I was living my values and doing what I love to do (leading and inspiring others), I met Paul. We are now married and living in a little seaside town in the south of England with our two adorable little girls. My dreams came true. And being with him *is* just like breathing—effortless, but I couldn't imagine life without him.

From working with clients and from more than enough of my own experience, I can say with certainty that if you don't know what your emotional needs are they will *run* your life and, left unchecked, can potentially *ruin* your life. And, if you aren't living your passions and values, you are missing out on a great way to effortlessly attract the relationship you want. So if you have tried the flirting books and the rule books and are now brave enough to go deeper and find out what might be getting in the way of finding the person of your dreams or discovering the love that somehow got lost in your current relationship, this is the book for you. Shall we get to work?

1

....

The Secret of
Irresistible Attraction

Y EARS OF COACHING thousands of people to reach their goals has taught me that there is one factor that makes all the difference in attracting and maintaining great relationships. People who have great relationships have figured this out consciously or unconsciously. The secret to being irresistibly attractive to your current or potential mate is to fulfill your unmet emotional needs and live your top core values.

After working on her personal and emotional needs, one of my clients, a senior executive at a major financial institution, was completely and utterly astounded and asked, "Why hasn't anyone ever mentioned emotional needs before? Why isn't this common knowledge?" She couldn't believe that something so essential to her happiness and success in life, not to mention in love, was something she had never heard about before. Why is this a big secret? I had to agree that very few people talk about their personal and emotional needs, for two reasons: (1) they aren't aware they have them, or (2) if they are aware, they don't want anyone to know about them. We think that if we don't talk about our needs, no one will notice them. Ha! In this book, you'll learn not only what your top four personal and emotional needs are, but also how to fulfill them so that they effectively disappear.

The Law of Attraction is that thoughts manifest reality. What you think about is what you attract. Like attracts like. As Henry Ford wisely said, "If you think you can or if you think you can't, you are right." The flip side to that is that if you are focusing on lack you'll attract more lack because what you focus on expands. And if you resist your situation by denying it, ignoring it, or simply being unconscious or unaware of it, it will get worse because what you resist persists. You can't ignore your debt and expect it to magically disappear. These are the fundamental laws of attraction. *Like attracts like.* The obvious corollary to that law is this: *If you don't need it, you are more likely to attract it.* Any form of neediness is incredibly repellent—the greater your sense of lack, the greater your need, the more likely you are to repel the thing you want most.

We all know at some level that neediness in any form is inherently repellent. Have you ever been at a party where someone was chatting with you and you couldn't wait to get away from him? You probably made up some excuse like having to get a drink in an effort to get away. You couldn't say precisely, but something about this person makes you want to end the conversation as quickly as possible. Well, that something is usually an unmet need.

I know what you are thinking: "I'm not like that. I'm not needy." But what you may not realize is that *all* human beings have personal and emotional needs and unless you know what your specific needs are, you are probably walking around with some unfulfilled needs. Most of us are. I certainly was.

Even incredibly smart and successful people have unmet needs. I remember reading an article about Jane Fonda's divorce from Ted Turner, one of the wealthiest and most successful people in the world. She said he was "too needy." It doesn't matter how successful you are; if you don't know what your needs are and how to fulfill them, you will be, at some level, emotionally needy. And although people who don't know you well might not notice, your partner or mate will. So even the happily married will benefit from working this program and discovering their personal and emotional needs. If you are unhappily married, this book could very well be your salvation. In fact, one of my clients, a recently divorced business consultant and mother of two children, said, "If I had only known about my emotional needs sooner, I could have saved my marriage."

Most of my clients are very successful people (high-level corporate executives, business owners, government officials), and many of them have been happily married for years. They couldn't believe the difference that knowing and fulfilling their needs made in all their relationships, especially with their loved ones and families. It is the secret to being irresistibly attractive. It is the law of attraction: when we don't need someone, we are more likely to attract someone. The more you need someone or something, the more likely you are to repel that person or thing. Not fair, but definitely true.

If you have unfulfilled needs, you can't be irresistibly attractive no matter how good-looking you are or how much money you have. Remember, even Ted Turner with his good looks and money couldn't hang on to Jane Fonda. Fortunately, the reverse is also true. People who have fulfilled their personal and emotional needs are very attractive even if they don't have much in the looks or money department. They radiate a sense of confidence and self-awareness. We want to be around them. They are confident and emotionally mature. They don't need us, so they are around simply because they want or choose to be.

As a culture we have collapsed the notions of love and needs into one entity. Most people think that if someone needs you, that is good. That means they love you. Not true. Love can only be freely given. You can't force or require someone to love you. You can only attract love. Our needs, on the other hand, are requirements. We *must* get them fulfilled in order to be our best. For that reason, needs and love are incompatible. The best way to attract a man or woman is to *not* need them. How do you do that if you are a lonely singleton? You work this program until you completely fulfill your needs and are living your top values and passions on a regular basis. Then, you'll be irresistible. You'll also be more likely to attract the mate that you really *want*, not the one you think you need.

By the way, these principles apply to business as well. If you want to attract better people and opportunities, get your needs met. It really is that simple. However, I'll warn you right now, this program is not easy. It is the hardest coaching work my clients have to tackle. Once they've done it, however, they never go back to living the old way. Life is so much easier and more satisfying when our needs are fulfilled. In this book, I've made the rather difficult process of identifying and fulfilling our personal and emotional needs as simple as possible. There is even a quiz that you can take in about twenty minutes that will tell you what your top four needs are. And I've provided numerous examples of how my clients have fulfilled the most common twenty-one needs, which you can use to find ways to meet your own needs.

This isn't the sort of book you can just read and expect to reap all the benefit. You will have to do the exercises to get the results. And, at some point in the program, you will probably bump into resistance. You won't want to do it and you'll have all sorts of good reasons why these assignments don't apply to you. This is the challenge: it is precisely because you don't want to do the work that you have the unfulfilled need in the first place. If you didn't resist, then you would have satisfied that particular need ages ago. Resistance is actually a good sign that you've hit on a real need. So rejoice at the point when you are ready to toss this book out the window. That is when you need it the most! And, of course, I've included some advice on how to break through resistance.

The good news is that you can fulfill all your personal and emotional needs once and for all. And, contrary to popular opinion, you don't need your partner or mate to do it for you. In fact, the best way to attract and keep a mate is not to need one.

Once you fulfill your emotional needs, you'll be ready for the fun part of the program—discovering and living your top values and passions in life. This is when life gets really exciting and interesting. Let me guess, you're thinking you'll just skip the needs bit and go right for the fun stuff. Wrong! You can do this, of course, but here is the danger: your unmet needs could very well come back and bite you in the butt. Or, they simply might deprive you of feeling satisfied in life. One client, a retired CEO, happily married with grown kids, confessed that in spite of all his success in life, he was never really satisfied. It never felt like enough. Underneath it all lurked a rankling discontent. He had it all—money, career success, a good, happy family, a loving wife, travel—but for some reason, he still wasn't satisfied. He didn't realize that he had never fulfilled his emotional needs. Being unaware of his needs, they ran his life. One of his needs was to be the best, so he used to be the first one in the office and the last to leave, even if that meant waking up every morning at four o'clock to get to the office by six. Needless to say, he wished he had learned about his personal needs earlier. For one thing, he would have gotten a lot more sleep!

While many people struggle to get through the personal and emotional needs work, they all love doing the values work. We are naturally drawn to our values. Most people dream about having the time one day to fully express their values and passions. In this book you'll learn how to identify your core values and passions in life—the things you can't wait to wake up to do each day, whether that is creating, leading, managing, inspiring, peace, spirituality, beauty, adventure, fun, or play. Ideally, you want to restructure your life so that every day you can fully express at least one of your top four values. Your values are related to your purpose in life. It is what you were born to do and what you love to do. They give you energy, immense joy, and a profound sense of fulfillment. If you aren't aware of your values or haven't set up your life to live them, your life is half-lived. It is like having the cake without the frosting—not nearly as good as it could be. Don't make the mistake of waiting for a mate to start really living your life. When you are fully express-ing your values, you are incredibly attractive—downright irre-sistible, in fact.

Once you are living your life to the fullest and your needs are met, you'll find that you will attract all sorts of great peo-ple and interesting opportunities. You'll need to learn how to handle the power of irresistible attraction and how to accept all the good things coming your way. Most people unconsciously block the very things they say they most want. You might find that you sabotage your success in subtle ways. One recently unemployed client said he wanted more money. Yet, when he found a twenty-dollar bill on the sidewalk of New York City, he felt so uncomfortable about accepting this gift from the universe that he gave it to his roommate. That same week, he was house-sitting for some friends and they left him an enve-lope with some cash as a thank-you. He told them thanks for the kind offer, but he couldn't accept it. I guarantee you that if you do the work of this program, good things will come your way, but you must also learn to say yes to the things you want. You can sit right next to your future mate and miss him or her altogether for the same reason. We are so used to having to work hard for everything we have in our lives that we think if it comes to us easily, we aren't meant to have it. Or it is "too good to be true" so we don't trust it. Contrary to what you may believe, life is meant to be easy. It doesn't have to be such a struggle, but you must learn to accept graciously when you start effortlessly attracting what you've always wanted.

In the last part of the book, I'll share some tips on being simply irresistible that work for everyone—married or single, male or female. And, for those single women who are eager to find a mate and procreate, Chapter 10 contains the basic rules of dating and a time line so that you find your mate sooner rather than later, especially for women with an eye on the biological clock ticking relentlessly away.

The best way to attract and maintain a great relationship is to not need one and to be living a glorious life with or without the person. If you aren't totally thrilled with your life, then there is work to do!

2

· · · · · · · ·

The Eight Myths About Needs

ONE OF THE biggest mistakes you can make is to treat your personal and emotional needs as if they are optional. They are not. You simply cannot be your best if your needs are not fulfilled. I didn't figure this out for myself. This concept comes from the late psychologist and researcher Abraham Maslow, who describes the process of human growth and development as a hierarchy of needs. He has written numerous books and studied this for years, so I'm not doing him justice by reviewing his theories in one short paragraph, but the basic idea is as follows:

Maslow's Hierarchy of Needs

1. Physical needs (for example, food, shelter, clothing, and safety)

2. Emotional needs (for example, love, appreciation, and community)

3. Values and peak experiences (for example, adventuring, creating, and playing)

Maslow points out that as we progress and grow as human beings, our needs evolve. Our first requirement is to make sure we've got survival handled—our physical needs for food, clothing, shelter, and safety. Then, once we've done that, we start scouting around for emotional satisfaction and love. This explains why men don't usually pop the question until they feel secure in their careers. They need to make sure their survival needs are met first. Next, once our emotional needs are fulfilled we naturally look at our values and passions. We are then in a position to have really great lives oriented entirely around what we love to do.

Most people try to skip the emotional needs step in human development and go right for the fun part, the peak experiences. This is dangerous; if you don't first fulfill your needs, they will always come back to haunt you and you may struggle to live your values to the fullest. To live the best life possible and attract the best people to you, first and foremost focus on fulfilling your needs so completely that they effectively disappear.

Fulfill Your Needs to Become Irresistibly Attractive

· · · · · · · ·

There is a huge benefit to getting your needs fulfilled: you will instantly become much more attractive. This is one of the laws of attraction: *If you don't need it, you are more likely to attract it.* You've already experienced this in life. The man or woman you aren't interested in can't stop calling. You don't need them or aren't interested, so they are irresistibly drawn to you. Similarly, we all run from the classic "clinging vine," be they male or female. If you are too needy you'll turn your date off or scare him or her away. This principle also applies to business. If you have loads of credit card debt and go to the bank for a debt consolidation loan to get yourself out of debt, it is highly likely the bank will decline your request due to "excessive obligations." In other words, you are "too needy" or desperate financially. I used to be a bank manager and this is precisely what we did. On the other hand, if you had some savings, even with a poor credit rating, we would simply secure your savings and give you the loan. You don't need it, so we were happy to give the money to you.

To become more attractive to the people, love, and opportunities you most desire, you must banish all vestiges of neediness. And, to do that, it certainly helps to know specifically what your unique personal and emotional needs are and take practical steps to fulfill them in healthy, positive ways.

Instead of pretending our needs don't exist, we must do the opposite. We must figure out exactly what our personal and emotional needs are (there are many more than Maslow's original seven or eight) and then set up a system to automatically fulfill them. When I'm working with my coaching clients we work through each of Maslow's steps in the hierarchy of needs. First they'll take the Emotional Index Quiz to begin the personal and emotional needs process; next they'll identify their core or true values and peak experiences. Knowing what the process is and having specific programs to work on accelerates the process of growth and development. What a wonderful world it will be when we all get to the values part! So hurry up and get your needs met so we can all get on with the fun stuff in life.

Unmet Needs Rear Their Ugly Heads

· · · · · · · · ·

It is unmet needs that often drive people to do things that they know are not good for them (overeating, overspending, talking too much, being too bossy or controlling, being insecure, etc.), yet somehow they can't seem to stop. It is the unfulfilled needs that make a person appear needy and repel the very person and opportunity that is most desired.

Let's look at a classic example of how needs drive us to unattractive behaviors such as being insecure or overeating. Take Lauren, a twenty-seven-year-old, successful, professional marketing executive who always seemed to be falling in love with men who weren't interested in her. Her goal was to lose weight and get in shape so that she'd be more attractive to men and find the love of her life. To this end, she was always on a diet. No matter what she did, she always seemed to gain the weight back. She blamed herself for a lack of willpower. But I knew that beneath most bizarre behaviors (and by that I mean a behavior that you persist in doing even though you know intellectually or rationally it isn't good for you) there usually lurks an unfulfilled need. It is the unfulfilled need that keeps the behavior in place because needs aren't optional. We will do anything to try to fill our needs, even things we know aren't good for us. While just about everyone agrees that humans have a need to be loved, most people have only a vague idea of what their specific personal and emotional needs are. Do you have the need to be cherished? Appreciated? Valued? Adored? Heard? In control? For peace? Order? Most people are not aware of their key needs and very few people (not even Maslow) have a good system for figuring out specifically what those needs are or how to get them fulfilled in healthy ways.

I worked with Lauren to figure out what unmet need was driving her to overeat. She discovered that one of her top needs was for security. She would eat whenever she felt insecure or unsure of herself. Of course, the excess weight only made her feel more self-conscious and insecure. Food was not the answer, and trying to diet was only attacking the symptom, not the source of the problem. Once Lauren realized that she was eating to feel secure, she started working on feeling secure in other ways. We discovered that she didn't have any savings—hmmm . . . was the excess fat her emergency reserve? She started an automatic savings plan to create a six-month reserve of living expenses. What else would make her feel secure? Lauren was an extremely sensitive person, and if someone made a rude comment or remark to her, she didn't know how to respond. She'd simply feel terrible and reach for some pastries or cookies for solace. Lauren learned to use a simple, four-step communication model if anyone made a hurtful comment or remark to her (see Chapter 5). This made her feel more secure because she now knew how to protect herself from verbal slights. Immediately Lauren felt more confident and she noticed that she wasn't reaching for the pastries as often. With her key emotional need fulfilled, and stronger boundaries in place, Lauren started attracting really great men who liked her just the way she was. Once she realized she was attractive with the extra weight and didn't need to lose weight to attract a good man, the weight started coming off. When we don't *have* to do something it is more likely to happen—one of the laws of attraction. What you resist, persists. Lauren didn't need to lose weight so it now came off naturally. Most people, like Lauren, work their goals in reverse. They think they need more money to get what they want, or need to lose weight to attract the right partner, when in fact all they need to do is fulfill their needs and live their values. If you do this, you will effortlessly attract the right people and opportunities into your life.

Before we move on to figuring out what your personal and emotional needs are, let's blast through the most common myths about needs that could be holding you back from finding the love of your life or keeping the love you have.

Blasting the Myths

. . . .

Neediness is unattractive at best. If you are looking for the man or woman of your dreams, it makes sense to eliminate anything that might make you less than irresistible. Just as you might get rid of an unsightly wart or mole before embarking on your quest for Mr. or Ms. Right, you must rid yourself of any vestiges of neediness to be as emotionally attractive and appealing as possible. Whether you are consciously aware of your needs or not, they do exist. To need is normal. So, you might as well face the facts and learn the true nature of your needs.

Myth #1: It's Bad, Weak, or Unattractive to Have Needs

Most people assume that having needs or being needy is undesirable and unattractive. This belief exists partly because we value self-reliance and independence. But, more than that, we have all experienced how unpleasant it is to be around someone who is overly needy.

The Truth: To Need Is Human. This is a really important distinction: having needs and being needy are not the same. While it can be unattractive to have unfulfilled needs, having needs in itself is not a negative trait. All human beings have needs. Just as it isn't good or bad to have the need to eat, neither is it good or bad to have the need to be in control or the need to be held tenderly, the need to be heard, the need to be appreciated, or any other emotional need. Just because someone does not appear needy doesn't mean that that person doesn't have needs. Those who appear confident, as though they don't have needs, are simply better at getting their needs fulfilled. The good news is that everyone, no matter how needy, can learn to fulfill his or her needs—if you know exactly what those needs are. The problem is that most people have only vague notions of what they need. But we'll get to that later.

Don was a high-powered regional director of a major construction firm and had the need to be in control. He came to me because he had been unlucky in love and wanted to find a stable relationship, and we started talking about his life at work. His boss, a micromanager, was always stopping him from making independent decisions, which irritated him to no end. His boss was giving Don accountability but removed his authority by not letting him make important decisions without his approval. Don didn't want to admit to his boss that he really needed to be in charge because he feared he'd look like a power monger. He felt his need to control was inappropriate and certainly didn't want to tell his boss about it for fear of appearing after his boss's job. After a bit of coaching, Don was persuaded to talk to his boss and tell him he really needed to have the authority to go with his accountability. They rewrote some of the procedures that had required his boss's signature so that he could sign off himself. This helped alleviate most of Don's dissatisfaction with his job. He eventually took this one step further and set up his own business so that he could always be in control and has been a happy camper ever since.

In Don's case his need didn't fully "disappear" until he fully satisfied it by becoming completely autonomous. Now that he runs his own business, he is in charge, which is completely appropriate. Once fulfilled, his need is now an asset and makes him *more* attractive, not less. Few people would enjoy working for a boss who didn't want to take charge or was reluctant to make decisions. Same need, just two different scenarios—once fully satisfied, the need is no longer a problem or a bad thing. And in fact, Don met a wonderful woman soon after he got his own business up and running, and they're now happily married.

Myth #2: The Love of Our Life Should Fulfill All of Our Needs

My clients are always telling me, "If he really loved me, he would not only know what my emotional needs are, but he would meet them all without my asking." Women are particularly guilty of this myth. It somehow got packaged into the notion of romantic love that our partner/spouse/love of our life/soul mate should intuitively know what our emotional needs are and then, because he or she loves us, naturally fulfill our needs forever, without our having to say a thing. This is absurd!

The Truth: Most People Can't Even Articulate Their Own Needs, Let Alone Figure Out What Someone Else's Needs Are. Here's a pop quiz: What are your top four personal and emotional needs?

1. _____

2. _____

3. _____

4. _____

Most people are stumped by this question and some can come up with one or two.

How specifically do you get these needs fulfilled?

1. _____

2. _____

3. _____

4. _____

Most people can come up with one or two needs, such as to be loved, to be heard, or to be appreciated (all fairly common needs), and then they have no idea what they or someone else could say or do *specifically* to fulfill that need for them.

So, how on earth can we expect another person, who has a completely different set of needs, to figure out our needs when we don't even know what they are? And yet, we go into relationships with this HUGE unspoken expectation. No wonder most relationships are ultimately disappointing. The source of disappointment is an unfulfilled expectation.

Let's look at Isabella, a busy working mother, MBA, and former high-powered executive at a prestigious consulting firm. She stopped working at the firm after her first child was born, has been married now for six years with two small children, and started running a small business from her home. Isabella came to see me and admitted that she was already starting to resent the children and her husband. She realizes this has to do with the fact that she now has two small children and doesn't have the same amount of free time she had before. She figured this was just the way it was going to be until the kids got older and more independent. We talked about it and she realized that one of her core needs is to be unrestricted. If our needs are not fulfilled, we simply can't be our best, so waiting for the kids to grow up is just not an acceptable option. She agreed.

How can she fulfill her need to be unrestricted and still be a working mom? She had already hired a nanny, enabling her to focus on her business, but this still didn't give her any personal time. I asked her what she could ask her husband to do to help her meet this need. She admitted that she had hoped he would volunteer to help without her asking him, but that wasn't happening. I told her she could be waiting a long time for him to think of what to do, or she could simply make a request and see what he said. What she really wanted was for him to take the kids for an occasional weekend so that she could get some time away with friends. And, during the week, to sit with the kids for an evening or two while she went out for a bike ride. It had never occurred to him that she felt restricted. When she asked for his support and made these specific requests, he was happy to oblige. Now Isabella is much happier, even though she still has the same obligations of work and family. A little bit of unrestricted time for herself has made all the difference.

Myth #3: Asking for It Ruins It

Many people believe that if they ask someone else to fulfill their needs, it will spoil it. They think that if they have to ask for what they want, when they do receive it, getting it won't be as satisfying—kind of like knowing what your Christmas presents are before you've opened them.

The Truth: If You Don't Ask, You May Be Waiting a Long Time. It simply isn't true that asking someone to fulfill your needs ruins it. In fact, the opposite is true. Unfortunately (or perhaps fortunately!) our mates can't read our minds, so sometimes the *only* way you'll get your needs met is to make a specific request of your partner. I am thinking of one couple in particular. Susanne was adamant that if she asked her husband, Dan, to meet her need to be loved and complimented, that it would spoil the compliment. On the spot, I had her turn to Dan and tell him, "When you tell me I'm beautiful, I really feel loved." She did this, turning bright pink with embarrassment in the process. And then Dan said, "You are a truly beautiful woman." She blushed crimson at this point. I asked Susanne if she felt the need was fulfilled in that moment and she said yes, but it still seemed insincere and fake to have to ask. A year later I heard from Dan that she was asking him to meet her needs all the time now! She got over it.

So there you have it. Asking for it does *not* ruin it. It feels just as good—or even better, because now you'll feel more powerful. You'll have to try this for yourself before you'll really believe me. It is much more attractive to ask directly and specifically for what you need rather than to slink around coyly trying to coax it out of someone. For example, if you want your boyfriend to tell you that he admires you, don't ask, "What do you think about me?" Instead say, "Tell me what you like about me." You are much more likely to elicit the response you want. If you are turning in a project at work to your boss and you want to know what he likes about it, don't ask, "What did you think of this report?" Instead say, "Tell me what you specifically liked about this report."

If you haven't asked your own children to meet your needs, you are missing out because kids are great at doing it and they love it! One client, Melinda, a corporate executive, mother of two girls, eight and thirteen years old, told her daughters that she had a need to be appreciated and loved and asked each of them to tell her each night before they went to bed what they most appreciated about her or loved about her. The youngest told her that she loved her very much and appreciated the way she always read a bedtime story. The next day she made a special card out of construction paper and glue and gave it to her mother at bedtime. The elder daughter told her that she was the best mom in the world. At the end of the week, Melinda was overwhelmed with the amount of love and appreciation she received from her daughters. They so enjoyed doing this that it has now become a nightly habit, and she tells her girls what she appreciates about them as well. She also gave her daughters a wonderful gift by showing her girls that it was natural and normal to have needs and to tell the people you love how to fulfill them.

Myth #4: Asking Will Make Me Appear Even Needier

I often hear clients say, "I don't want to ask because then people will definitely *know* that I'm needy." The myth here is that if we don't draw attention to our needs by talking about them, people won't know we have them.

The Truth: Asking Makes You Appear More Confident. You can't hide neediness; we instinctively sniff out neediness a mile away, so pretending you don't have needs isn't fooling anyone. Neediness and any form of desperation reek! It's much more appealing and powerful if you just come right out with it. In fact, it is refreshing.

Asking people to meet your needs makes you appear more confident. You probably won't believe this until you've tried it, so start by observing people who ask very directly and specifically for what they want. They tend to have no trouble getting their needs fulfilled because they are in the habit of asking for what they want and need.

Lisa realized she had a need to be heard. When she was sharing a story or issue with her friends or spouse, she would get frustrated if they jumped in right away with their advice or offered suggestions. At first, Lisa didn't feel comfortable asking people to meet her needs. She found herself getting into arguments with co-workers who wouldn't let her speak, and she was constantly irritated with her boyfriend, which of course made her unpleasant to be around. After much prodding, I finally convinced her to get over her fear of appearing needy, and Lisa decided to tell people exactly what she needed from each of them. At work, Lisa gently informed her boss and co-workers when she wasn't finished with a thought. She held her ground firmly. As a result, her boss and colleagues learned not to interrupt her and she gained respect, and ultimately a promotion.

On the home front, Lisa got in the habit of letting her boyfriend know when she just wanted him to listen. "Honey, what I really need from you right now is ten minutes of pure listening. Would you be willing to just listen to me, without saying anything?" Lisa said her piece and felt heard. She reported that the whole experience was gratifying instead of frustrating. She thanked her boyfriend for listening and told him how much she appreciated what he'd done. He felt good because he was able to make her feel better and got some appreciation as well. He learned that he didn't have to try to solve her problems or to offer suggestions or advice because what she really needed was someone to listen to her in a nonjudgmental way. Instead of appearing needy, Lisa appeared more confident because she was willing to ask directly for what she wanted.

Myth #5: Do Unto Others as You Would Have Them Do Unto You

OK, I am fully aware I'm treading on sacred ground here. This is the Golden Rule, after all. It applies to the big rules in life: Don't steal from someone because you don't want your stuff stolen. Don't beat someone over the head because you don't want your head bashed in. Don't sleep with your neighbor's wife unless you want your neighbor to sleep with your wife. The Golden Rule makes a great deal of sense with the big stuff, but it falls apart when applied to our needs and wants. It leads one to the natural assumption that if you love to be lavished with gifts and chocolate, then so does everyone else.

The Truth: Do Unto Others as They Want Done Unto Themselves. The more people I have worked with, the clearer it becomes how very different everybody is. Yes, all humans have the need to eat, but some like mayonnaise and some don't. Any good host knows that just because she likes goose liver, doesn't mean that her guests will like it. The best host takes into careful consideration her guests' dietary preferences. Joe is a vegetarian, so I'll make sure to have plenty of vegetable dishes, and Rhonda is allergic to shrimp, so I'll serve that as an appetizer instead of a main course so she can avoid it. This is a thoughtful host—one who is aiming to please her guests and make for a great evening for all involved.

The same goes for our emotions. Just because you might have the need to be appreciated doesn't mean that all your friends do as well. Perhaps what your best friend really needs is to be included. So instead of wasting your breath appreciating her, you would make her much happier by simply calling to invite her to join in activities, even when you know she is busy and can't attend. The call to include her is what she really needs. True, all humans have emotional needs, but some have the need to be heard, some have the need to be in control, some have the need to be taken care of, some have the need to share, some have the need for order. We are all different. And it is in appreciating and recognizing the differences that we live together peacefully and happily.

Maggie, a very warm and personable woman, is an extrovert. She has been happily married for years to an introvert. While she gets energy from others and needs to be connected to people, her husband, Frank, gets energy from being alone and needs peace and solitude to recharge his batteries. Most people make the mistake of assuming what is good for the goose is good for the gander. Not Maggie. She knows that she needs to be surrounded by people and loves a good chat. When friends and family are over, at some point Frank invariably gets up and excuses himself from the room to go off and read a book. Maggie has always encouraged him to do this. While some people might say, "Oh, don't be a party pooper!" and encourage Frank to stick around, or worse yet, criticize him because he wants to spend some time alone, Maggie knows that he can only stand so much. As much as he loves his family and friends, being around people drains his energy. Maggie has always been supportive of his need for peace and solitude. She's never made a big deal out of him getting up to leave and as a result, her friends and family accept it as well. And she doesn't deny her own needs either. She is perfectly happy to travel alone or with another friend if her husband doesn't wish to accompany her. She has a vital social life and includes her husband as much as he wants, but doesn't expect him to keep up with her. This is a great example of how two people with diametrically opposing needs can be perfectly happy together if they respect each other and don't expect the other person to have the same needs.

Myth #6: Real Men Don't Have Needs

There is another cultural myth that is running rampant and that is that men shouldn't have needs. We want men to have only two needs—the need to love and be loved and the need to be in control. And that is about it. I realize this is a gross generalization and of course there are millions of exceptions, but ask around and you will discover that most women don't feel comfortable when they discover that their man actually has some needs.

Culturally, we grant women the right to have more needs than men. Male clients are often reluctant to admit that they have a need to be adored, cherished, or taken care of (that sounds too feminine!).

The Truth: Men Have Just as Many Needs as Women Do. Needs are not inherently masculine or feminine, good or bad, better or worse. Real men have needs and aren't afraid to get them met. In fact, the more bold and direct they are about getting their needs fulfilled, the stronger and more attractive they appear and become.

Mark had the need to be adored and taken care of, and he loved being the center of attention. A very handsome man, Mark got into theater and acting, which handily fulfilled his needs when he had work, but he found the countless auditions and numerous rejections undermining. He had a few early successes in acting, but not enough to really generate a reliable career or a steady income. As a result he gave up acting and took up painting. Again, it was the same story: after initial positive reviews of his work, he found he couldn't make a living from selling his paintings and found it too hard of a struggle. He couldn't bear the negative criticism. He finally found his niche in computers where he could not only get appreciation for his talents but also make a decent income.

In relationships, Mark seemed to attract wealthy older women who admired him for his youthful good looks and very willingly spoiled him with their money. He enjoyed being taken care of, driving around with them in their fast, flashy sports cars, and living a luxurious lifestyle. This fulfilled his need to be adored, admired, and taken care of very nicely, except that he couldn't stand being thought of as a "boy toy."

Once he found a reasonably lucrative career in computers, he didn't need a woman to take care of him financially and was able to end those relationships.

Our needs can keep us trapped in relationships until we fulfill them. Once Mark got his needs fulfilled in his career, he could end the bad relationships and find the true love he was seeking. Now that Mark has a stable career and has bought a home, he has attracted a woman he loves for who she is, not for what she can provide. He has finally found real happiness in love.

Myth #7: We Are Our Needs

It is easy to assume that we are defined by our needs. For example, you might describe your friend, boss, or colleague as a "controlling person" when he has the need to control. Or say your manager is "bossy" if she has a need for power. Or someone is a "perfectionist" if he has the need for order or perfection. Or a friend is incredibly "thoughtful" or "generous with her time" when she has the need to be appreciated or thanked.

The Truth: We Are Not Our Needs, but We Can Become Them if We Don't Fulfill Them. Our underlying needs are so powerful that they can end up defining us if they aren't fulfilled. For example, if you don't find healthy and fulfilling ways to meet your need to control, you will be seen as controlling. Unfulfilled needs can take over our lives and define us in negative ways. Wouldn't you rather be defined by your values? Instead of being controlling, you could be an "inspiring leader." Instead of being a perfectionist, if you fulfilled your need for order, you could be known for your creativity or passion for excellence. Consider Martha Stewart. She is a perfectionist who fulfills her need for order while orienting her life around her values for creativity and beauty. Her life is bigger than her need for order; it is about her values. She doesn't deny her need, but instead makes her perfectionism part of the beauty. And, even if your manifestation of a need looks like a good thing, such as a need for appreciation driving you to send out countless notes and cards to friends so that you get some back in return (this is all done subconsciously), wouldn't you prefer to send out notes and cards because you want to, not in the hopes of getting some cards back? On the surface, the actions might not change, but your underlying motivation will. Take the man who was driven to be at work before everyone else and stay the latest so that he would be seen as "the best." If he had known about his need and had that fulfilled by friends, family, and colleagues acknowledging him, he would have had more time to be with his young children instead of missing their childhood altogether. The goal is to fulfill your needs completely so that you can orient your entire life around your values.

Myth #8: Having Needs Is Unpleasant

Most people think that not only is it bad to have needs, but it is unpleasant and painful as well. And it can be. If you are starving and have the need to eat, it is very painful and unpleasant and can kill you if you don't fulfill this physical need. If you are single and lonely because you can't find or attract a relationship, that hurts as well. But that's not the whole story.

The Truth: Having and Fulfilling Your Needs Can Be Pleasurable. Needs in and of themselves are not bad or unpleasant. Although neediness has gotten a bad rap, it can be very pleasurable and enjoyable to satisfy your unmet needs *if* you have the means readily available for fulfillment. When I'm traveling in a foreign country, there are so many restaurants and different foods I'd like to try I'm always disappointed when I get full and just can't eat anymore. I'd love to try something new, but I can't because I'm not hungry. Hunger is a welcome and pleasant need to have if you are surrounded by delicious food and have the means to partake. However, if you are hungry and there is no food to be had, this is a serious problem and being hungry isn't fun or pleasurable at all. The same goes for our personal and emotional needs. It is a pleasure to be loved and to love, but if you don't have a partner to share your love with, this need to love can leave you feeling lonely and sad.

Our sexual needs work in similar ways. When we have a loving partner, it is almost too easy to get our sexual desires fulfilled and our desire may start to fade. This is a perfect example of how once we have a system in place that makes needs gratification easy (a loving partner), the need itself seems to disappear. This can be why absence makes the heart grow fonder. One woman I know has a great, really sexy, exciting relationship with her husband, and this is partly because he is often traveling and away for months at a time. When they reconnect, it is like a honeymoon each time. Deprivation of needs makes them stronger while regular satisfaction can make them seem to "disappear."

Let go of these eight big myths about needs and you will be much happier and more attractive. Now let's find out exactly what your top four needs are by working through chapters 3 and 4.

3

....

Identify Your Needs:
The List Method

A T THIS POINT you are probably itching to figure out what your own personal and emotional needs are. The quickest and easiest method is to take the Emotional Index Quiz in Chapter 4 or at Lifecoach.com, which will tell you what your top four needs are. Or, if you prefer to study the entire list of needs, you can select your own needs from the list in this chapter. Identifying your needs is the first step in understanding how your needs are running (or possibly ruining) your life and to effortlessly attracting the love of your life.

While most people find it much easier to identify their needs with the Emotional Index Quiz, some people prefer to see the entire list of needs to choose from. The drawback to selecting your needs by studying the list alone is that you may find you skip over particular needs because you don't like the sound of them. For example, many women don't like the idea that they might have the need to control because it doesn't sound very feminine or attractive. Likewise, few men would feel comfortable circling the need to be adored, as it doesn't sound very strong and masculine.

The Needs List

· · · · · · · · ·

Grab a pencil, then study the list below. Scan the list and circle all the needs that resonate with you. It doesn't matter whether you circle the needs listed in bold or the needs that come after. Everyone has almost all of these needs to one degree or another, so don't worry if in looking at this list you freak out and say, "Geez, I've got almost all these needs!" Remember, to need is human. It isn't bad to have numerous needs. In fact, it is perfectly normal.

Personal and Emotional Needs List

1. **Accepted/Liked:** Approved of, Allowed, Endorsed, Included, Respected, Popular, Validated

2. **Achieve:** Accomplish, Attain, Complete, Get Results, Implement, Realize

3. **Appreciated/Valued:** Acknowledged, Complimented, Esteemed, Flattered, Thanked, Honored, Praised, Prized, Worthy

4. **Clarity:** Certainty, Exactness, To Know, Be Informed, Simplicity, Surety

5. **Control/Power:** Administer, Authority, Be in Charge, Command, Conduct, Direct, Dominate, Guide, Govern, Handle, Influence, Lead, Manage, Mastermind, Order, Preside Over, Regulate, Supervise, Superiority, Stamina, Strength

6. **Heard/Communicate:** Be in Touch, Connected, Convey, Impart, Listened to, Make a Point, Make Contact with, Share Yourself, Tell Stories, Be Understood

7. **Independent:** Autonomous, Free, Not Obligated, Self-Sufficient, Self-Determined, Unattached, Unrestricted

8. **Integrity/Honesty:** Authenticity, Forthright, Factual, Genuine, Loyalty, Openness, Sincerity, Truthful

9. **Loved/Cherished:** Adored, Admired, Desired, Held Fondly, Liked, Preferred, Relished, Treasured

10. **Luxury:** Abundance, Comfort, Cozy, Ease, Indulgence, Prosperity, Relaxed, Restful

11. **Order:** Checklists, Cleanliness, Discipline, Neatness, Organization, Perfection, Plans, Regularity, Routines, Structure, Tidiness

12. **Peace/Balance:** Agreements, Be Alone, Calmness, Harmony, Reconciliation, Serenity, Silence, Tranquility, Quiet

13. **Recognized:** Acclaimed, Admired, Applauded, Celebrated, Cheered, Commended, Get Attention, Get Credit, Glorified, Honored, Known, Noticed, Be Seen

14. **Responsible:** Accountable, Commitments, Duty, Do the Right Thing, Justice, Loyalty, Have a Mission or Cause, Be Devoted, Obliged, Pledge

15. **Right:** Be Deferred to, Correct, Not Mistaken, Morally Right, Understood

16. **Security/Safety:** Assurances, Commitments, Guarantees, Insurance, Protection, Reliability, Stability

17. **Supported:** Be Attended to, Cared for, Embraced, Given Gifts, Encouraged, Helped, Looked After, Nurtured, Provided for, Saved, Treasured, Taken Care of, Welcomed

18. **Touched:** Caressed, Connected, Cuddled, Held, Hugged, Kissed, Massaged, Stroked

19. **Useful/Needed:** Care for or Look After Others, Give, Be Helpful, Indispensable, Serve

20. **Win:** Be First, Be the Best, Conquer, Defeat, Master, Overcome, Persuade, Succeed, Take the Prize, Triumph, Vanquish, Victory

21. **Work:** Be Busy, Be Industrious, Do Tasks, Exercise, Have a Career or Vocation, Labor, Make It Happen, Perform, Produce, Take Action

Now that you've selected a number of needs from the list above, try to narrow it down to four key needs. The way to do this is to ask, "If this need were fulfilled, would it take care of any of the others?" It's like bowling. If you knock down the kingpin, it takes the other pins down with it. Our needs work the same way, so don't panic if you've got a big bunch of them. You'll discover that once you take out the bigger needs, a number of others are naturally and effortlessly handled in the process. So go for the big ones!

For example, let's say you've looked at this list and have circled to be loved, cherished, adored, held fondly, complimented, given gifts, and appreciated. Of these, is there one word that sums it all up for you? For example, if you were adored, would that include being loved, cherished, held fondly, and given gifts? Pick the word that most resonates with you and feels the most encompassing. Whichever you choose, that will be one of your kingpin needs. If you focused your efforts on getting that one need fulfilled, the others in that category would happen naturally. The main category may or may not be the word that personally resonates with you, so pick the word that does. Now that you've reviewed the above list, select your top four personal needs and write them below. If you have a need that isn't on this list, feel free to add it. Just make sure it is a requirement for you to be your best.

Top Four Needs (The Kingpins)

1. _Loved (Cherished)   (Supported, Touched_
2. _recognized (Appreciated, Accepted_
3. _Heard/Communicate_
4. _achieve   (Work)_

Let's take Britanny, the thirty-something manager of a retail store, as an example. Britanny came up with the following top needs:

1. To be cherished (kingpin need including to be loved, liked, held fondly, adored, get compliments and gifts)

2. To be independent (kingpin need including to be free and not obligated)

3. To share (kingpin need including to be heard, communicate, and tell stories)

4. To have balance (kingpin need including peace and harmony)

The "Opposite" Approach

Rather than counting up the number of times you marked a certain need, you can also try the "opposite" approach. Look at the list of needs above and see if you have strong negative reactions to any of the words. Is there is a term you definitely *don't* want to be one of your needs? Is there one that would feel too embarrassing or weak to have? If so, circle that one. The words we strongly avoid are often unmet needs. It is because you instinctively avoid it or are afraid or reluctant to admit that you might have that need that you don't seek to fulfill it. You certainly wouldn't tell anyone it was one of your needs and you might even deny it vehemently. Such unfulfilled needs result in "neediness." Remember, no need is any better or worse than another. It isn't better or more noble to have the need to be cherished than the need to be right. Please be honest with yourself. Once your needs are fulfilled, they will effectively disappear, so it won't matter whether you like the need or not.

The "Not Your Best" Approach

Because needs are a requirement for you to be your best, when you aren't your best or arc cranky and irritable, look around for an unmet need. One client found himself getting very irritable with his spouse when he came home from work and the house wasn't tidy. He had the need for order and the clutter bugged him. He would spend the first few minutes running around putting things away before he could relax. Once his partner realized he wasn't irritated at her, she would spend a few minutes tidying the house before he came home and avoided the problem altogether. We can't be our best if our needs aren't fulfilled.

The "What You Do for Others" Approach

Here is another way to uncover your needs. Sometimes we subconsciously do for others what we'd like to receive ourselves. We have been taught that if you want to be loved, then give love. If you want to be complimented, then give someone a compliment. This is fine, but it would be much better if you did what the other person needed instead of doing what you needed. For example, one of my clients would send me little notes of appreciation a couple of times a week. Now I thought that was very nice, but a bit excessive. In fact, I felt a bit burdened by all these notes, thinking I needed to send her one in return. So I asked her if she sent notes like this out to everyone in her life. She said, "Yes." Aha! I asked her if she had the need to be appreciated. Again, her answer was yes. There we had it. She was sending out scads of notes as a means to get one or two back to fulfill her need to be appreciated. Instead of doing all this work, I suggested she simply ask people directly for what she wanted. She asked me to e-mail her a note of appreciation once a week. She also asked her parents to call her and tell her what they appreciated about her as well as to send her the occasional note. She saved all these notes in a pretty floral box and would read them when she felt in need of a little appreciation.

The "Second Opinion" Approach

If you are in doubt, ask a partner, family member, or good friend to help you identify your needs.

"Honey, do you think I have a need to be in control?"

"Yep."

People who live with us or know us well can usually spot our needs right away, so once you've selected your top four, you can review them with your partner. Our friends and family may not be able to consciously articulate what it is you need, but once presented with the need, they can confirm whether it is a need of yours or not. But be careful as sometimes people will unconsciously impose their own needs on you. To avoid this problem, just take the quiz as it isn't biased.

If you are struggling to pick your needs out of this list, good! I hope you are beginning to see how ridiculous it is to assume that your romantic partner should meet all your needs when it isn't particularly easy to pull them out of a list yourself. You can stop struggling and go ahead to Chapter 4 to take the Emotional Index Quiz to identify your top four needs, or, if you feel confident that you have established your top four needs, you are ready to move on to the needs fulfilment process which begins in Chapter 5.

4

. . . .

Identify Your Needs: The Quiz Method

The easiest way to identify your needs is to take the Emotional Index Quiz online and get a report of your top four needs. This quiz was developed with the collaboration of the coaches at Lifecoach.com, a team of some of the most highly trained, effective coaches in the world. We noticed that clients really struggled to identify their needs from a list, so we came up with a very simple quiz to help them quickly and effortlessly determine their top four needs. While the quiz isn't flawless, it has been developed over years of experience with hundreds of clients and works in a natural, organic way. If you prefer to do things online, go to emotionalindex.com and follow the instructions. If you don't have Internet access or prefer to do things on paper, you can take the paper and pencil quiz that follows and score yourself. (The quizzes are identical.) Be honest. Remember, to need is human. We *all* have needs, and those who appear as if they don't have simply done a better job of getting them fulfilled.

Paper and Pencil Emotional Index Quiz

· · · · · · · ·

Instructions: Read the scenarios below. If the situation rings true for you, check the corresponding need that most resonates with you. You are looking for the underlying need that drives the behavior. If the scenario isn't true for you or wouldn't apply to you, just skip it and move on to the next scenario. If the scenario is true for you, but none of the needs listed sounds right, then skip it. You will probably skip quite a few that don't apply. On the other hand, don't worry if you have checked a large number; that is perfectly normal as we all have needs, some more than others. If you aren't sure about a question, ask a friend or family member who knows you well how they think you'd answer.

1. You need a balance of work and play in your life in order to feel your best. If you work too much, you lose your sense of humor. If you play too much, you tend to get lazy or apathetic.

   ☑   Need for balance.

2. You are at a party and two people start to argue. You feel uncomfortable and either try to smooth things over or shy away from the conflict.

   ☐   Need to be accepted/liked.
   ☑   Need for peace/harmony.

3. You are always doing favors for other people, even at your own personal expense.

   ☐   Need to be accepted/liked.
   ☐   Need to be appreciated.
   ☐   Need to be useful/needed.

4. You keep others at arm's length. You don't want to get hurt.

- ☐ Need to be accepted.
- ☐ Need for safety/security.

5. You go out of your way to help others, even though you don't really have the time.

- ☐ Need for peace/harmony.
- ☐ Need to be useful/needed.
- ☑ Need to be responsible/do the right thing.

6. You are constantly sending thoughtful notes, cards, or gifts to family, friends, and colleagues.

- ☐ Need to be appreciated.
- ☐ Need to be accepted/liked/included.
- ☐ Need to be loved/cherished.

7. You hate being interrupted.

- ☐ Need to be heard/listened to/communicate.
- ☐ Need for control/power.

8. People don't take what you say seriously.

- ☐ Need to be heard/listened to/understood.

9. You feel like you are drowning—there are so many things vying for your attention that you have no time to pursue your true calling.

- ☐ Need for order.
- ☐ Need for balance/peace.
- ☐ Need for clarity.

10. You get irritable and cranky if your home is messy.

- ☐ Need for order/tidiness.
- ☐ Need for clarity.

11. You can't think clearly until your desk is cleaned off.

- ☐ Need for order/tidiness.
- ☐ Need for clarity.

12. You find yourself volunteering in the community at a homeless shelter, the church, or some other charitable organization, but your family doesn't appreciate all you do for them and the work you do in the community.

- ☐ Need to be needed/useful.
- ☐ Need to be appreciated/liked/approved of.
- ☐ Need to be responsible/have a cause or mission.

13. When your boss micromanages you, you feel suffocated. You think, "Why can't she or he trust me to do the job right?"

- ☑ Need to be independent/free.
- ☐ Need to be accepted/respected.
- ☐ Need for power/control/authority.
- ☐ Need to be right/deferred to.

14. It annoys you that your spouse/partner doesn't do things for you, such as loading the dishwasher, unless you ask him or her.

- ☐ Need to be cared for/supported/taken care of.
- ☐ Need to be loved/cherished.

15. You feel (fill in the blank) when your spouse or partner does small things around the house without your asking.

- ☐ Cherished/loved.
- ☑ Supported/taken care of.

16. You get anxious or restless when you don't have a project to work on. You enjoy pushing the limits to see what can be done.

- ☑ Need to accomplish/achieve.
- ☐ Need to be busy/work.
- ☐ Need to have a cause or mission/responsible.

17. You get frustrated with bureaucracy that slows you down from getting results.

- ☐ Need be free/independent.
- ☑ Need to accomplish/achieve.
- ☐ Need for power/control/authority.

18. You find yourself eating out of the fridge or in front of the TV even though you are not really hungry.

- ☐ Need to be cherished/loved.
- ☐ Need to be nurtured/supported/taken care of.
- ☐ Need for security/safety.
- ☐ Need to be busy/work.

19. People don't appreciate your point of view. You make a statement and nobody seems to hear you or understand you.

- ☑ Need to be heard/listened to/understood.
- ☑ Need to be recognized/get attention.
- ☑ Need to be appreciated/valued.

20. You always have to have the remote control.

☐   Need to be in control/power.

21. You can't stand it when your boss or colleague takes credit for what you've done.

☐   Need to be recognized/get credit/noticed.
☐   Need to be appreciated/acknowledged.

22. You get very frustrated and/or upset if you don't get the recognition you deserve at work.

☐   Need to be recognized/noticed.
☐   Need to be appreciated/acknowledged/valued.

23. You feel lonely and removed from people and lose the desire for sex when you are not in a relationship.

☐   Need to be touched/held.
☐   Need to be loved/cherished.

24. You get furious, hurt, angry, or disappointed if you find out your friends make plans without inviting you, even if you know you can't attend. You want to be invited anyway.

☐   Need to be included/liked.

25. You get really upset or annoyed if people do things or make plans without your knowledge.

☐   Need for power/control.
☐   Need to know/clarity/be informed.

26. You have plenty of money in the bank, but you still don't feel secure. It is never enough somehow.

- ☑ Need for security/safety.
- ☐ Need for luxury/comfort.

27. Nobody loves losing, but you *really* can't stand it. You have to win, even if it is just Monopoly or a card game for fun.

- ☐ Need to win/be the best.

28. People say that you are too opinionated or bullheaded because you have to get your point across.

- ☑ Need to be heard/communicate.
- ☐ Need to be right/understood.
- ☐ Need to be responsible/do the right thing/duty.
- ☐ Need to win.

29. You have been known to tell your spouse or partner which way to turn out of the driveway.

- ☐ Need to be in control.

30. You like it when your boss, family, and friends approve of what you do and find it disturbing if they don't.

- ☑ Need to be accepted/approved of.
- ☐ Need to be appreciated/valued.

31. At parties and social gatherings, you need to be the center of attention and will tell jokes, sing songs, do silly stuff, or wear clothes that are guaranteed to attract attention.

- ☑ Need to be recognized/get attention/be seen/noticed.

32. You find it hard to do nothing and prefer, even when on vacation, to work on some project or another.

- ☐ Need to be useful/needed.
- ☑ Need to accomplish/achieve.
- ☐ Need to be busy/work.

33. If you don't have at least ten minutes of quiet time a day to yourself, the rest of the day is off kilter.

- ☐ Need for peace/balance/be alone.

34. It is vital for you to be in a position of power or authority. You need to be the one in charge whether at work or at home.

- ☐ Need to be in control/power/authority.

35. You can't be in a relationship unless your partner/spouse is faithful to you. An open marriage wouldn't work for you.

- ☐ Need to be in control/power.
- ☐ Need for responsibility/duty/loyalty.
- ☐ Need to be loved/cherished.

36. You are a perfectionist and can't abide it when things go afoul.

- ☐ Need for perfection/order.

37. You find yourself shopping several times a week. You get a high from shopping, but then feel guilty afterward because you are buying on credit and know you can't pay off your credit card balance. Still you continue to shop, knowing you really shouldn't.

- ☐ Need to be loved/cherished.
- ☐ Need for luxury/comfort/abundance.

38. You go into restaurants even when you are not planning to eat there, just to see if anyone you know is dining there.

☐ Need to be seen/admired/recognized/known.

39. You can't sleep at night unless you've checked to make sure all the doors are locked.

☐ Need for safety/security.

40. You have a stockpile of canned goods and household supplies on hand.

☐ Need for luxury/comfort/abundance.
☐ Need for security/safety.

41. You feel compelled to always do the right thing, no matter what.

☐ Need for honesty/integrity.
☐ Need for duty/responsibility/justice.

42. Although you hate to admit it, you don't go on a second date with a person if he or she didn't pick up the tab on the first date. You much prefer being treated and feel that your date can't be all that interested in you if he or she didn't treat.

☐ Need to be supported/cared for.
☐ Need to be loved/cherished.

43. You love gossip. You can't resist passing on a juicy tidbit.

☐ Need to be recognized/get attention/known.
☐ Need to be included/accepted/liked.
☐ Need to be heard/communicate/tell stories.

44. You naturally expect people to bring presents to your birthday party and feel miffed if someone doesn't bring one.

☐   Need to be cared for/supported.

45. You would never eat at a restaurant where the service was lousy, even though the food was superb.

☐   Need to be cared for/attended to/supported.
☐   Need for luxury/comfort.

46. You need to know that your lover/partner/spouse desires you. It isn't enough that he or she says so. You want demonstrable evidence before you are satisfied.

☐   Need to be supported/cared for.
☐   Need to be touched/caressed.

47. You tend to find yourself in messes or problems, but fortunately, someone comes along to rescue you or help you out.

☐   Need to be saved/supported.

48. You often ask leading questions in order to get a compliment, such as, "How do you like my dress/suit/hair?"

☐   Need to be loved/cherished/desired/adored.
☐   Need to be admired/recognized.
☐   Need to be complimented/appreciated.
☐   Need to be supported/encouraged.

49. You need a commitment before you can do your best work or be your best self—whether that is a job contract or a marriage contract.

☐   Need for security/safety.
☐   Need for clarity/certainty.

50. After a bad day, nothing makes you feel better than being held tenderly.

- ☑ Need to be touched/held.
- ☐ Need to be supported/cared for.
- ☑ Need to be loved/cherished/desired.

51. Life feels blah if you don't have a cause to rally behind.

- ☐ Need to be responsible/have a cause or mission.
- ☐ Need to accomplish.
- ☐ Need to work/be busy.

52. You frequently write letters to the editor to correct injustices and wrongs.

- ☐ Need to have a cause or mission/duty/be responsible.
- ☐ Need to be right.
- ☐ Need for honesty/integrity.

53. You have to have the last word in an argument.

- ☐ Need to be right.
- ☐ Need to win.
- ☐ Need for power/control.

54. You can't stand being wrong.

- ☐ Need to be right.
- ☐ Need to win.

55. You go the extra mile when you have someone to encourage you.

- ☐ Need to be useful/needed.
- ☐ Need to be supported/encouraged.

56. Puns annoy you.

☐ Need for clarity/certainty.

57. You prefer to give rather than receive presents because you don't want to feel obligated.

☐ Need not to be obligated/to be independent.

58. You always have extra presents on hand to give as gifts.

☐ Need not to be obligated/to be independent.

59. You feel compelled to tell all and reveal everything even when it probably isn't in your best interest to do so at times.

☐ Need to share yourself/communicate/be heard.
☐ Need for honesty/integrity.

60. You refuse to take money from your friends or family, even though it would make your life easier.

☐ Need not to be obligated/to be independent.

61. You can't stand taking orders from someone else.

☐ Need to be independent/free.
☐ Need to be in control/power.

62. If an error occurs, you quickly take responsibility, even if you were only partially at fault or not at fault.

☐ Need for duty/responsibility.
☐ Need for honesty/integrity.

63. You can't stand working on projects that you can't complete yourself.

- ☐ Need to accomplish.
- ☐ Need to be in control.
- ☐ Need for perfection/order.

64. You love lists and make them every day. You get joy from checking things off a list.

- ☐ Need for clarity.
- ☐ Need for order/checklists.
- ☐ Need to accomplish/achieve.
- ☐ Need to work/be busy.

65. If you don't meditate every day, you can't function at your peak.

- ☐ Need for peace/balance/be alone.

66. Your favorite days are jam-packed from start to finish. You relish the sense of accomplishment.

- ☐ Need to be busy/work.
- ☑ Need to accomplish/achieve.
- ☐ Need to be useful/needed.

67. You always go above and beyond the call of duty at both work and social occasions.

- ☐ Need to be useful/needed/indispensable.
- ☐ Need to be valued/appreciated.
- ☐ Need to be recognized.
- ☐ Need to win/be the best.

68. You volunteer to cook dinners for the local church group or soup kitchen.

- ☐ Need to be needed/useful.
- ☐ Need to do the right thing/duty/responsible.
- ☐ Need to be valued/appreciated.

69. You donate a lot of your time and energy to charities or environmental organizations.

- ☐ Need to be needed/serve.
- ☐ Need to be responsible/duty/do the right thing.

70. You need to have all the facts before you are comfortable making a decision.

- ☒ Need to be informed/clarity.
- ☐ Need for security.

71. You tend to break the rules or make up your own rules.

- ☐ Need to be free/independent/unrestricted.

72. You are at a company banquet, and, rather than see all the leftovers go to waste, you ask the waitstaff to bring you a few containers so you can take the leftovers home.

- ☒ Need for security/safety.
- ☐ Need for comfort/abundance/luxury.

73. You will work extra hours if you know that your boss values your efforts.

- ☐ Need to be appreciated/valued.
- ☐ Need to win/be the best.
- ☐ Need to be approved of/liked.
- ☐ Need to be admired/recognized.
- ☐ Need to be supported/encouraged.

74. You would never ask for a doggie bag to take home the leftovers at a fancy restaurant. It just wouldn't look good or be cool.

- ☐ Need to be accepted/liked/respected.
- ☐ Need to be admired/recognized.

75. You prefer to eat food that comes in its own neat little package (yogurt, bananas, frozen dinners, instant oatmeal).

- ☐ Need for order/perfection.

76. You always balance your checkbook every month to the penny.

- ☐ Need for order/perfection.
- ☐ Need for clarity/certainty.
- ☐ Need for security/safety.

77. You tend not to speak up at a party if you know your views would cause an argument.

- ☑ Need for harmony/peace.
- ☐ Need to be approved of/liked.

78. You get really irritated when people don't confirm receipt of your e-mails or phone calls.

- ☐ Need for clarity.
- ☑ Need for acknowledgment.
- ☐ Need to be recognized.
- ☐ Need to achieve/accomplish.

79. You never leave the house without making sure your hair looks good, your makeup is on, and you are well dressed.

- ☑ Need to be admired/recognized.
- ☐ Need for order/perfection.
- ☐ Need to be appreciated/complimented.

80. You proudly display all the awards, plaques, certificates, or other forms of reward, recognition, or achievement in your home or office.

- ☑ Need to be important/recognized/admired.
- ☐ Need to be respected/accepted.

81. You feel treasured when your mate holds your hand, whispers sweet nothings in your ear, or makes other intimate gestures. If he or she doesn't do these things, you feel something is missing or he or she doesn't really like you.

- ☑ Need to be cherished/loved/treasured.

82. You love to get gifts. It doesn't have to be anything big; little presents and surprises are great! If you don't receive them from a loved one, you feel a bit neglected or unloved.

- ☐ Need to be cared for/supported.
- ☑ Need to be cherished/loved.

83. You enjoy parties and going to social events on occasion, but find you really need some time alone to recharge. You may have to step outside for a breather at large social events.

- ☐ Need for peace/balance/be alone.

84. At holidays and other family gatherings, you get exhausted by the socializing and usually need to go out for a walk alone, or leave the room to read a book or watch TV.

☐ Need for peace/balance/be alone.

85. You don't like asking for directions and hate being told where to go by backseat drivers.

☐ Need to be in control.
☐ Need to be right.

86. You tend to get obsessed with whatever you are currently doing, but find you are actually happier and more productive if you balance work and play.

☐ Need for balance.

87. You don't like it when people touch you, even though you know they mean well or are just trying to comfort you.

☐ Need to be in control.

88. You love getting and giving hugs. You frequently reach out to touch someone's hand or arm, especially if they are feeling sad or hurt.

☑ Need to be touched/held.
☐ Need to be loved/cherished.
☐ Need to be supported/taken care of.

89. When you throw a party or event, you always make sure to include everyone. You know how horrible it is to be left out.

☑ Need to be accepted/included.
☐ Need to be loved.

90. If you make a mistake, you take it very hard, even personally.

- ☐ Need to be right.
- ☒ Need for perfection/order.
- ☐ Need to be the best/win.

91. You need people to be perfectly clear and can't stand it when they mumble or ramble on.

- ☐ Need for clarity.
- ☐ Need for perfection/order.

92. You always say what is on your mind, even though it isn't always appropriate.

- ☐ Need for honesty/integrity.
- ☒ Need to be heard/communicate.
- ☐ Need to be right.
- ☐ Need to be responsible/do the right thing.

93. You get upset, concerned, or angry if someone doesn't fully communicate with you. You'd rather know the truth even if it is hard to hear.

- ☒ Need for honesty/integrity.
- ☐ Need for clarity.

94. When traveling, you take along all the comforts of home. In fact, you'd rather not travel if you can't be comfortable.

- ☐ Need for comfort/luxury.

95. You find you must keep the upper hand in most situations.

- ☐ Need to be in control/power.
- ☐ Need to be right.
- ☐ Need to win/be the best.

96. It's your way, or you'll find someone else who will do it your way.

- ☒ Need to be in control/power.
- ☐ Need to be right.
- ☐ Need to win.

97. You are known as the person who gets projects completed on time.

- ☒ Need to achieve/accomplish.
- ☐ Need to be recognized/known.
- ☐ Need to win/be the best.
- ☐ Need to work/be busy.

98. You don't respect people who are disorganized or messy.

- ☐ Need for order/perfection.

99. You must do your duty to your church, family, and country.

- ☐ Need for duty/responsibility.
- ☐ Need to be useful/needed/serve.

100. While some people seem to thrive on noise and chaos, you really can't think clearly or work effectively in a noisy environment.

- ☐ Need for peace/harmony/balance/be alone.

101. You always tell the truth, even though it might be easier or better not to.

- ☒ Need for honesty/integrity.
- ☐ Need to be responsible/do the right thing/justice.

102. You would never take even so much as a postage stamp from the office for personal use.

- ☐ Need for honesty/integrity.
- ☐ Need for duty/responsibility.

103. You make a concerted effort to fit in, regardless of the situation.

- ☐ Need to be accepted/liked/approved of/included.

104. A balanced life? That's for wimps!

- ☐ Need to be busy/work.
- ☐ Need to accomplish/achieve.
- ☐ Need to win/be the best.

105. You are overly generous and insist on treating friends and family, even though you really can't afford it.

- ☐ Need to be appreciated/liked/valued.
- ☐ Need to be cherished/loved.

106. If you are out to dinner with a date, you insist on paying your way, even if your date wants to treat you.

- ☐ Need to be free/independent/not obligated.

107. You have to be the boss, even if that means owning your own business or company.

- ☐ Need for power/authority/control.
- ☐ Need for freedom/independence.

108. You play full out to win. You don't let others beat you if you can help it.

- ☐ Need to win/be the best.

109. You aren't a very gracious loser. You really hate losing and have a hard time disguising the fact.

☐ Need to win/be the best.

110. You prefer to drive, even if it isn't your car.

☐ Need for control/power.
☐ Need to be free/independent/unrestricted.

111. You don't feel loved if your partner doesn't cuddle up to you or caress you.

☐ Need to be touched/caressed.

112. When stressed, you usually pick up the phone and talk things over with a friend.

☐ Need to be heard/communicate.

113. Your friends say you have a fear of commitment, but you are really afraid of losing your independence or control.

☐ Need to be free/independent.
☐ Need for control/power.

114. You can't stand it if your partner reads the paper at mealtimes instead of talking or listening to you.

☐ Need to be heard/communicate.

115. You often reach out and touch people.

☐ Need to be touched.

116. People may say that it is the thought that counts, but you aren't impressed by small tokens or trinkets. You want your loved ones to give you real jewelry or expensive gifts.

- ☐ Need for luxury/abundance.
- ☐ Need to be cared for/supported.

117. You often come up and give your partner a hug or massage his or her shoulders while he or she is at the computer.

- ▨ Need to be touched/caressed.

Scoring Instructions

· · · · · · · ·

Once you've finished answering questions, go back and add up how many times you've checked a particular need. For example, you may have checked "approved of" three times, "cherished" twice, "control" three times, and so forth. Now go back to the List of Personal and Emotional Needs in Chapter 3 and look up your top four needs. Is there another word that resonates more or sounds more encompassing? For example, you might have the need to be accepted, but, when you study the list, you actually decide it is more accurate to say you have the need to be included. List your top four needs here:

Top Four Needs

1. _loved/cherished/protected/held_
2. _heard/understood_
3. _recognized/attention_
4. _accepted_

Congratulations! You have completed the first step in getting your needs met—knowing what they are! At this point you might feel completely comfortable that these are in fact your top four needs, in which case, you can move on to Chapter 5 and start setting up systems to fulfill them once and for all so that they "disappear." Or, you might be curious and want to double-check (in which case you probably have the need for clarity or certainty!). Go back and review the list of needs in Chapter 3 to verify your top needs.

5

· · · · · · · ·

Establish Boundaries

NOW THAT YOU are fully aware of your top four personal and emotional needs, the next step is to figure out how to satisfy them once and for all so that they effectively disappear. There are two steps in this program, and while they are simple to follow, you may not find them easy to do.

First, you will expand your current boundaries, putting in place even bigger boundaries than you think you need. This will give you a greater sense of confidence and provide the added benefit of making you much more attractive to potential and current mates. We are naturally attracted to people with firm and clear boundaries, and we can't help but treat them with respect. Boundaries are also the key to true intimacy. Without boundaries it is impossible to be truly intimate because it isn't safe enough. If you are, at some level, worried about getting hurt, you'll put up barriers to protect yourself or keep people at a distance.

Second, you will learn how to ask directly for what you need. As I mentioned in Chapter 2, this flies in the face of the commonly held belief that asking for what you want spoils it. The best way to get your needs met is to be very specific and clear about what you want others to do and say.

You will also create an automatic system to permanently and effortlessly satisfy your top four needs. Initially, there is work to do to put the system in place, but once established, you will reap the benefits for the rest of your life.

After completing the exercises in this section, you will be much more attractive to your soul mate (whether you are married or single) and will have eliminated any neediness you may have had, whether you were consciously aware of it or not. The exercises that follow are challenging and you may resist doing them. I encourage you to do them, *especially* if you don't feel like it, because that is precisely where you will gain the greatest benefit. If it were easy you wouldn't have these needs in the first place; you would have already fulfilled them. Put in the effort now and you will be rewarded with a profound sense of inner satisfaction and confidence that may have eluded you all your life.

Establish Bigger Boundaries than You Think You Need

The first step in getting your needs fulfilled is to put firm boundaries in place to make sure you are treated with respect. Without sufficient boundaries, you have no chance of fulfilling your needs permanently. A boundary is like a moat around the castle in that it is designed to protect you from unfriendly attackers. To put it simply, a boundary is something that no one may do to you or around you. Most people already have boundaries in place, even if they aren't aware of them. For example, most people have the boundary, "People can't hit me." If someone hits them, they'd call the police and immediately end the relationship. This is a very basic physical boundary. Some people, however, don't have this boundary and stay in relationships where they continue to get hit.

A bigger boundary than "No one may hit me" is "No one may yell at me." This is one step out from physical abuse to verbal abuse. One step further from "People can't yell at me" is "People can't make rude remarks about me or put me down." And then further still, "People can't give me unsolicited criticism." And even further, "People can't be angry, grumpy, or argue with others around me."

You can make up and have any boundaries you wish. The bigger they are, the better. You need much bigger boundaries than you realize. List the ten boundaries you would like to have. Here are some basic and typical examples to get you started:

- People can't hit me.
- People can't yell at me.
- People can't give me unsolicited criticism.
- People can't argue or fight in my presence.
- People can't be crabby or grumpy around me.
- People can't interrupt me.
- People can't be late when meeting me.
- People can't make rude or derogatory remarks or jokes about me or those around me.
- People can't gossip around me.
- People can't take advantage of me in any way.
- People can't make racial jokes in my presence.
- People can't waste my time.
- People can't use my things without my permission.
- People can't lie to me.
- People can't use foul language in my presence.
- People can't be mean to me.
- People can't ignore me.
- People can't smoke in my home or around me.
- People can't call me before 9:00 A.M. or after 9:00 P.M.
- People can't interrupt my private or quiet time.

- People can't give me work they should do themselves.
- People can't belittle me or dismiss my remarks or opinions.
- People can't snap at me.
- People can't say things to me that make me feel stupid.
- People can't take out on me feelings/issues that they have with other people.
- Work cannot treat me inequitably.

You can choose any boundaries you like from this list and then add your own below. Take a moment to write down the ten key boundaries you want in your life.

My Top Ten Boundaries

1. _____

2. _____

3. _____

4. _____

5. _____

6. _____

7. _____

8. _____

9. _____

10. _____

At this point you are probably thinking, "Great! So I've got this new boundary, 'People can't raise their voice to me.' Now what do I do about it?"

Installing Bigger Boundaries

· · · · · · · ·

*"The way in which a person loses their true good-
ness is just like the way that trees are destroyed by the
ax. Cut down day after day, how can the mind, anymore
than the tree, retain its beauty or continue to live?"*

—MENCIUS, fourth century B.C.

I have taught thousands of people this extremely effective four-
step communication model for establishing your boundaries.
The first step is to realize that whenever someone crosses one
of your boundaries, you've allowed him or her to do so. If you
want the behavior to change, you need to let that person know
about it. The following is an example of how to stop the irritat-
ing or undesirable behavior in a graceful and effective manner.
(Ladies, pay attention, we tend to be particularly weak in this
department!)

1. **Inform.** For example, "Do you realize that you are yelling?" Or, "Do you realize that comment hurt me?" Or, "I
   didn't ask for your feedback." If the person continues with
   the unwanted behavior, take it to step 2, but only after
   you've tried step 1.

2. **Request.** Ask the person to stop. For example, "I ask that
   you stop yelling at me now." Or, "I ask that you only give
   me constructive feedback." If he or she still doesn't get it
   and the behavior continues, try step 3.

3. **Demand or Insist.** "I insist that you stop yelling at me
   now." If he or she still persists, take it to the next step.

4. **Leave** (without any snappy comebacks or remarks). "I can't
   continue this conversation while you are yelling at me. I
   am going to leave the room."

The key to success with these four steps is to say them in a neutral tone of voice. Do not raise or lower the volume of your voice. You know when you've got a little fire or judgment in your tone. Remember, you are informing the other person, so keep it calm. Think of going through the four steps in the same way you'd say, "The sky is blue."

What Do Boundaries Have to Do with Being Confident and Attractive?

· · · · · · · · ·

How can you feel good about yourself if people are yelling at you all day? How can you feel appreciated if people criticize you? It is very difficult to stay positive in these situations, especially if you are surrounded by criticism and negativity on a regular basis at home or at work. Even if it isn't personal, it just isn't acceptable for anyone to yell at you. Period.

When I worked at Chase Manhattan I was taught that good customer service meant allowing angry customers to vent their frustration and anger and then offering them assistance. During my six years in retail banking, I listened to customers complain and yell every day. I was drained and exhausted at the end of each day. A good day was one in which no one was upset. But, people didn't often come into the bank if everything was OK. Were customers' reasons for being upset valid? Yes, more often than not, they were. But that didn't mean that as an employee I had to be their sponge. This was a revelation to me and, to be honest, I was dubious whether boundaries could really work with the bank's customers. After all, the customer is always right.

As an experiment, I put in place the basic boundary, "People can't yell at me," and of course I was tested that very day. From my office at the back, I could hear a man yelling at my customer service representative. I immediately thought, "Here goes," and walked out to the counter where a forty-ish man, reeking of alcohol, was yelling at my rep. I approached him and in a neutral tone of voice informed him, "Do you realize you are yelling?" He was immediately flustered and, still yelling, said, "Of course! I'm not mad at you, though, I'm mad at the bank." "I understand," I said, "and you are still yelling. I ask that you stop yelling now so that we can help you." He mumbled something and walked to the teller window to conduct his business. When he had completed his transaction he went back to the customer service desk and apologized for yelling. Then he came to me and apologized as well. He left the bank a happy customer and as far as I know, he never yelled in our branch again. It worked! And if it could work on an inebriated, belligerent man, then it could work on just about anybody.

I taught my entire staff the four-step model for installing boundaries and told them I would back them up as long as they kept their voice completely neutral and calm. If they raised their voice to the customer or got angry, they were on their own. The atmosphere of our branch transformed in one week. Customers started to treat staff with respect. The branch became a pleasant place to work and went from being a madhouse to a quiet, tranquil place. I knew we had succeeded when a gentleman came in to tell me he chose to bank at our branch because it had the best atmosphere in the entire neighborhood.

Now you are probably wondering what this has to do with attracting a mate. Before my environment at work improved, I would come home needing a lot of cherishing from my boyfriend to compensate for the abuse I had taken during the day. My job was, in effect, making me even needier. And the man who was willing to put up with my neediness was needy as well. Like attracts like. So once I installed sufficiently large boundaries at the bank and didn't allow any customers to be abusive to me or my staff, I wasn't as needy. By fulfilling my need to be cherished from friends and family, I no longer needed my boyfriend to fulfill that need. I was able to see that he really wasn't the right man for me, and we broke up. By separating the needs from the relationship, I could see it more clearly and could end it and move on.

Unfulfilled needs can keep you stuck in a relationship that isn't right for you. Remember, we *have* to get our needs met and will do even illogical or self-destructive things in an attempt to satisfy them. If you find that you keep being drawn back into a relationship that you know isn't good for you, I would wager it is a case of your needs driving you to do it. Fulfill your need from other people who love and care about you and you will release the pull the relationship has had on you and you'll be able to move on.

Aren't Boundaries Controlling?

· · · · · · · ·

Some people are concerned that having boundaries is about controlling others. This is a free country. Aren't people entitled to do or say whatever they want? Yes, for the most part, they are, and you are entitled to choose whether or not to stick around. Boundaries are not about controlling others. People will do what they want. Boundaries are about protecting yourself from others. When you inform people, you are simply teaching them how to treat you.

Everyone has different boundaries. For example, it may not bother you if someone is late to meet you for an appointment, while it might infuriate another. Because people have different boundaries, it helps if you inform them of yours by gently telling them at the first infraction. Do not wait. It is much easier to stay calm and neutral if you address things immediately.

Gracious Ways to Inform People That They've Crossed a Boundary

"Do you realize that you are _____ (fill in the blank: ten minutes late, interrupting me, yelling at me, criticizing me, angry at me, being rude to me, ignoring me?)" Use a flat, neutral tone of voice when you are informing someone. Think of it as holding up a mirror and reflecting back to them what they are doing. Let them take the graceful exit and save face.

"So sorry, I had no idea of the time."

"Of course, I know you would always respect my time."

Ninety-five percent of the population will get the message and show up on time for your next appointment. And for those who don't, take it to level two—request. "I request that you show up on time."

People often make the mistake—especially women, since we have been raised to think we are being nice by not addressing something on the spot—of letting an infraction pass the first time. You might think, "Oh, this is just the first time," or, "It is just a small thing, so I won't make a fuss." In fact, this is precisely the time to inform. You might say, "This is our first appointment, so you had no way of knowing how important timeliness is to me." Or more simply, "I'd appreciate it if you show up on time." If you address the behavior immediately it is easier to do it in a neutral tone of voice without anger, resentment, or judgment. It is when we wait that all the anger builds and gets in the way of our ability to enjoy the relationship.

People treat you the way they do because you have allowed them to do so, and you must take responsibility for how you have trained and educated people. Make it easy on yourself and give others, especially the ones you love, a chance to change their behavior. Inform and request a couple of times with friends and family before you move to demand and insist.

Don't Boundaries Keep People at a Distance? Don't They Shut People Out?

Here we must make an important distinction. *Boundaries* are permeable and allow us to let the "good guys" over the moat and into the castle. It is *walls* that keep everyone out. If you don't have sufficient boundaries, you'll get burned and will eventually put up walls to protect yourself. Boundaries enable us to really open up and be intimate because we feel safe. The bigger your boundaries, the safer and more relaxed you'll feel and the easier it will be to deeply connect with other people. This is especially true in love relationships. It is essential to have clearly defined boundaries with your spouse, partner, and all your loved ones.

What if the Four Steps Aren't Working?

If the four steps aren't working, first check to make sure you are using a neutral tone of voice. You may not realize how easily a bit of anger or indignation can slip in. If you are certain you are using a neutral tone, then take the fourth step—leave the relationship. Ultimately, you can choose whether to continue that relationship or not. The good news is that I've never seen a case when honoring one's boundaries was not rewarded. Sometimes friendships and relationships or jobs will end, which creates the space for new and better people and opportunities to come into your life. I've had clients who decided to quit their jobs. For example, one woman's boss just didn't get it and persisted in making sexist and derogatory remarks about her. She quit and found a new job where people treated her with respect, and she made more money!

Setting boundaries is not about controlling other people. We can't control others and we can't force people to treat us in a certain way. However, with sufficient boundaries we can protect ourselves and choose what environments we stay in.

Won't I Seem like a Prima Donna Making All These Demands?

· · · · · · · · ·

Nope. Remember, to demand is the third step. First, inform and request before you demand. If you do so in a neutral tone of voice (not a demanding or righteous tone), then you'll engender respect. Even if people choose not to honor your boundaries, they will probably respect you more for having them. Start with the boundaries that are most important to you and work your way down.

Also, this isn't a one-way street. The flip side of boundaries is standards, the conduct we hold ourselves to. It isn't appropriate to have the boundary, "You can't yell at me" if you are yelling at others. Expanding your boundaries may have the benefit that you will also need to raise your own personal standard of conduct.

One client was very demanding of her boyfriends and had a very hot temper. She used to yell at her boyfriends and expected them to put up with her bad behavior. Finally, one boyfriend had strong enough boundaries and said it wasn't OK for her to yell at him for any reason. He wouldn't be in a relationship with anyone who treated him so badly. If she raised her voice, he immediately informed her in a gentle but firm tone. She got the message, respected him for it, and learned how to control her temper. His boundary required her to raise her own standard of conduct. She is no longer with this man for other reasons, but she is grateful for the lessons she learned from him.

Benefits of Having Strong Boundaries

· · · · · · · ·

Setting bigger boundaries is a stretch, but well worth the effort because of the rich reward: people will respect you. We respect people who have big boundaries and we do not respect those who don't. Indeed, we are often tempted to abuse those without boundaries. Perhaps it is part of the survival of the fittest concept—animals casting out the weak and sick so the stronger members can thrive. Like animals, we can sense boundaries immediately. This is good news. Often, the moment you install a new boundary, such as "People can't criticize me," you'll either be tested right away or no one will criticize you. People instinctively sense your new boundaries and don't go there. It is a powerful new aura that you'll be projecting.

Strong boundaries enable us to become less needy. We are naturally attracted to the people we like and respect—the people who have a sense of dignity and self-respect. When you have strong boundaries, it is easier to attract the right man or woman in your life. And, without them, it is impossible to maintain a healthy relationship.

Now that you have written down your top ten boundaries and have started informing those around you, you will find that you won't need as much. It is often our inadequate boundaries that create the need in the first place. For example, if you have the need to be respected and your friends and colleagues constantly show up late when meeting you or interrupt you when you are speaking, you might feel that they disrespect you. Once you have the boundaries in place, people will naturally treat you better. The better we are treated by others, the better we feel about ourselves. This is normal, natural, and completely effortless. And all it takes is a concerted effort up front to retrain and educate those around you about how you need to be treated going forward. Once you do this, you'll find it is easier to ask people to do specific things to fulfill your needs, which is the next step in the program.

6

· · · · · · · ·

How to Meet the Top Twenty-One Core Needs

A T THIS POINT you have identified your top four needs and are ready to get them fulfilled. Figuring out what your core needs are, what boundaries you'll need to establish, and what systems to put in place to fulfill your needs is an extremely powerful exercise.

Before You Begin: Prepare for Your Own Resistance

· · · · · · · ·

At some point you will probably resist the emotional and personal needs assignments with every fiber of your being. I know this because 99 percent of my clients have resisted working on their needs. It is *precisely* this resistance that stands between you and the relationship of your dreams. Resistance is actually a very good sign. It means you've hit on a real need. If it were easy, you would have already fulfilled that need. It is hard only because this need is still lurking about in the dark shadows like a hungry wolf.

A client of mine wrote, "I never realized asking five people to take care of my needs could be so difficult. It makes me feel very silly, vulnerable, unbalanced, sick, and incapable of taking care of myself. I guess asking people for help is just the opposite of what I normally do, which is taking care of others and helping them." If your resistance takes the shape of fear, that is also a good sign. The more afraid you are to ask someone to fulfill your needs, the more important it is to ask. This is about the growth of your soul. You will get through this and it will get easier. I promise. In fact, once you break through the barrier of resistance and ask one person to do one thing to fulfill one of your top needs, you might wonder what all the fuss was about.

Before You Begin: Pick a Needs Team

· · · · · · · ·

There are two ways to get your needs met: (1) you can ask other people to meet your needs, and (2) you can fulfill the need yourself. A word of caution: do not rely solely on yourself to meet your needs. It is no more appropriate than it is to rely solely on your partner. While some needs lend themselves to self-satisfaction quite easily, other needs don't. For example, you might easily fulfill a need for peace or balance by taking time to meditate, walk in the park, or journal every day, but it is very hard to feel appreciated if no one is telling you how wonderful you are and what they appreciate about you. It is a need you simply will have to ask for help with.

Think about who you can rely on to help fulfill your needs. Perhaps your mother is great at telling you how much she loves you. She would be a terrific candidate to ask to call you once a week to tell you how much she loves you or what she appreciates about you. If your best friend is a good listener you might ask her to go out to lunch with you once a week for the next eight weeks. You may find peace by meditating every day or doing yoga, and know that you can fulfill your own needs in that way.

Be wary of falling into the trap of only asking your romantic partner to meet your needs. It actually works much better if you get your needs met from everyone *other* than your partner. You probably already put too many expectations on your partner to fulfill your emotional needs. As one client said, "Whenever I think about who to ask to take care of my needs, the only people who come to my mind are my ex or potential boyfriends. It seems that I've only accepted 'help' and care from my partners, as they could not say no if they wanted to stay with me." She reluctantly admitted that her boyfriends eventually ended up leaving her. Even her friends and family agreed that she was putting too many expectations on the man in her life to make her happy. Once she started getting her needs met from her friends and family, she could enjoy her romantic partner for who he was, not what he could do to satisfy her emotionally.

Remember, fulfilling your emotional needs is not your partner's role or responsibility. It is your responsibility to get your own needs met by setting up a team of people who already love you to help.

Establish Bigger Boundaries Now

• • • • • • • •

In addition to setting up a needs team, you'll want to establish bigger boundaries. Where there is an unfulfilled need, there usually lurks a weak boundary or two as well. Ask yourself where is this need *not* being fulfilled in my life? Who isn't meeting this need for me? Have I told this person (or persons) specifically how to meet my need? Your answers will show you where you have weak boundaries that need to be expanded. For example, if your father always criticizes you, no matter what you do to try to please him, you are missing the boundary, "People can't criticize me." Ask yourself, "Have I told this person specifically how to fulfill my need?" If the answer is no, now is the time to do so! If your boss micromanages you and it is driving you crazy, this could indicate a need for freedom or independence. Again, strong boundaries are required. You'll need to educate your boss on how to treat you to get the best results from you. For example, you might try informing her with, "I do my best work when given free rein."

The Plan

· · · · · · · ·

The explanation of needs that follows is necessarily a generalization and a compilation of what my clients have done that worked for them. Your unique solutions may emerge from these suggestions or not. The important thing is to start experimenting with ways to meet your own needs once and for all. My hope is that seeing these examples will make it easier for you to come up with your own solutions and ideas. The needs below are listed in alphabetical order so that you can look up your top four needs easily.

1. Accepted/Liked
Approved of, Allowed, Endorsed, Included, Respected, Popular, Validated

If you have the need to be accepted, you like to know that your friends and loved ones consider you an important part of their lives. You might seek others' approval or respect and need to know that they think you are doing just fine and that they accept or approve of your choices in life. Some people might call you a people pleaser as you seek the acceptance and approval of people you admire and respect. In relationships, you'll feel most comfortable if your loved ones agree with your choices and approve of your actions. At work, you'll do best if you get the approval of your boss and colleagues.

If your need is to be included, you can't stand being left out. It isn't always logical, but it is true. For example, you want to be invited to a party or event even if the host knows you'll be out of town that week. You'd still like the invitation because it makes you feel included and a part of things. Because of this need, you are very sensitive to others and make sure to include people who might feel left out. You might notice someone standing alone at a party and approach him or her so that person will feel part of the group. You may be the one in your group of friends to say, "Don't forget to invite so-and-so." In relationships, you probably won't feel accepted until your date introduces you to his or her best friends and family or includes you in family events. At work, you like to be included in meetings and be part of committees that are important to you. If a group in the office is going out to lunch or happy hour, you want to be invited as well, even if you have to decline. You can usually satisfy this need at work by having strong boundaries in place and asking your manager to give you regular feedback and to include you in meetings or conferences that interest you.

Meeting the Need Through Others

- Ask your parents to write you a letter telling you that they accept you and approve of your choices and decisions in life even if they disagree with them personally.

- Ask your closest friends to send you a postcard once a week with one or two sentences describing what they like about you. If you want their approval for anything in specific, let them know.

- Tell your friends, family, or colleagues that you like to be included and to please invite you to dinners, parties, outings, meetings, and so forth, even when they know in advance you won't be able to attend. Let them know you don't want to hear about things you haven't been invited to as it makes you feel left out.

- Ask your boss for regular feedback on how you are doing. This can be in informal weekly or monthly meetings by phone or in person. Let him or her know this motivates you to work even harder. Don't wait for the annual review to find out how much your boss approves of your work and contributions.

- Tell your romantic partner how you'd like to be included. For example, if it is important to meet your partner's friends and family, let him or her know.

Meeting the Need Yourself

- Make a list of all the ways you accept, like, or approve of yourself. What are you proud of having accomplished in life? What do you like about yourself? Put this list and any cards and notes, letters of commendation, awards, and so forth, in a box to revisit whenever you wish.

- Ask if you can sit in the middle of the table so you don't get left out of the conversation.

- At home, use a round table so everyone is included in the conversation.

- Introduce yourself to people you don't know. For example, if your friend is chatting with someone they bumped into on the street, extend your hand and say, "Hello, I'm so-and-so."

- Ask your host or friend to introduce you to people at a party or event so you feel a part of things right away.

Meeting Your Partner's Need

- Tell your partner what you like about him or her and avoid all criticism even if it is indirect. In other words, if you are out to dinner and the asparagus is overcooked, don't mention it. Instead point out what you *do* like about the meal. Men in particular feel personally criticized by such a comment, even though they have no control over the asparagus.

- Invite your partner to events and activities even if you know that he or she won't be able to attend. Your partner likes being invited in any case and will appreciate the invitation.

- Make sure to introduce your partner to important friends and family as soon as you feel comfortable doing so and include him or her in family gatherings.

Caroline's Story. Caroline had the need to be approved of. She was embarrassed to admit it because she was a successful, thirty-something human resources professional and felt that she was mature enough to be past this need. She knew intellectually that she shouldn't need approval at this point in her life, but emotionally she still felt the need. She was living with her boyfriend of a few years and was hoping that he would propose to her soon. Caroline liked her work and her life and knew that she had made the right choices, but she still felt the need to be approved of. I reminded her that the only way to get past a need is to fill it. We worked out a strategy to get her need fulfilled from everyone except her boyfriend so that he wouldn't feel pressured or burdened by her needs in any way. She started with her father, since she felt the need for his approval the strongest. She asked him to send her a note once a week for the next eight weeks telling her something that he approved of about her. Her first week, she didn't get a note but a six-page epistle outlining all the things he thought she had done well in life and all her accomplishments. She was surprised that he had thought of things she hadn't even remembered. The letter was wonderful and she saved it to reread whenever she needed. She then asked her manager to tell her what she saw were her strengths at work and what she was doing well. Her boss took the time to put this in writing and, given the time to think about all that Caroline was doing for the department, realized she was due a pay increase. She put Caroline in for an unexpected raise. Caroline also asked two close friends and one colleague to e-mail her once a week for the next eight weeks with a sentence or two about one thing they thought she was doing well or liked about her.

All this approval felt great. For the first time in her life, her need was completely fulfilled and it freed her. She no longer needed approval from her boyfriend. Funny thing, out of the blue, without any prompting, he asked her to marry him! They have now been happily married for five years and have started a family. Whenever she feels the need crop up again, she simply gets out her box and reads all the wonderful letters, notes, and e-mails she received. Now that all her friends know what Caroline needs, they regularly fulfill it without her having to ask.

2. Achieve

Accomplish, Attain, Complete, Get Results, Implement, Realize

If one of your needs is to accomplish, you may be a high achiever and a go-getter. You are usually good at setting and achieving goals and like to be acknowledged for the results you produce. You may also be more task-oriented than people-oriented. As a result, you may fail to put the time you need into relationships and have a tendency to put work before fun. If your needs are met at home and at work, you can be proactive and attentive in relationships. In the workplace, you typically prefer to work with results-oriented people and managers and like to be rewarded and recognized for your achievements. You are willing to work hard to fulfill this need and usually focus on getting results in the work world more often than in your personal life. To get this need fulfilled, you might focus excessively on work to the point of becoming a workaholic. Neglecting your home life may show that you don't get a sense of achievement from mundane tasks such as washing dishes or fixing the garden hose. You might satisfy your need by making lists so you can check things off, feeling a sense of accomplishment as you do.

Meeting the Need Through Others

- Ask at least five family members, friends, or colleagues to tell you by note, card, call, or e-mail what they see as your most significant accomplishments in life.

- Ask your parents to write you a letter listing all your accomplishments, starting with your earliest childhood achievements. Get a letter from each parent if you can.

- Ask your partner to tell you one thing every day that he or she sees as an accomplishment. You might tell him or her about your day and then your partner can say something like, "Wow! You really accomplished a lot." Or, "I'm really proud of all that you do." "I appreciate the long hours you put in at the office today in order to provide for the family. Thank you!" Or, more specifically, "Good for you for finishing that report on time."

■ Ask your partner to make a list of the things he or she would like you to do, both romantic and mundane. For example, your partner may like you to cook dinners every Thursday night or give him or her a massage. In addition, ask your partner to provide you with the list of things you can do around the house—checking things off a list often provides you with a sense of accomplishment even for mundane tasks like doing the laundry or mowing the lawn or caulking the bathtub.

■ Ask your partner to reward you when you complete the list with something special that you'd like or with an acknowledgment or some appreciation.

Meeting the Need Yourself

■ Keep a box with all your letters of accomplishment and put any other reminders of your accomplishments in it as well (newspaper clippings, letters of recommendation, etc.) to review whenever you feel in need of a boost.

■ Do complete work. If "accomplish" is one of your needs, you may find you prefer to work on projects you can complete. You might find it frustrating to work on only a portion of a project and never know the end result.

■ Focus on what is important. It is easy to get caught up in the workday—answering e-mails, writing memos, fielding phone calls—and can feel as if you really aren't accomplishing anything. If this is how you feel, try this tip from my first book, *Coach Yourself to Success*: When you are planning your day, either in the morning or the evening before, get out a sheet of paper and write down the answer to the following three questions:
  – What is important about today?
  – What *must* get done today? (Only the absolute musts.)
  – What is important about the future?

Focus exclusively on this list and you will feel an amazing sense of accomplishment.

- Define success for each day. One client decided that he would fulfill this need by deciding every day what his *one* accomplishment would be. Whether that was to take the day off to celebrate his son's birthday or to make sure he took the car in for servicing, he made sure that he accomplished that one thing and then he felt good about the whole day.

- Keep a running list of your accomplishments. Once you sit down to think about it, review your diary, and make a list, you'll realize you have accomplished quite a bit. If you don't take time to list your accomplishments, you may feel as if you aren't doing much.

- Highlight your accomplishments. One CEO has the need to accomplish. He meets this need every day by highlighting all the things on his to-do list with a yellow marker as soon as he finishes the task. His goal is to have a completely yellow page at the end of the day. I like this approach because it emphasizes his accomplishments, not what he hasn't done. This tiny positive reinforcement serves as motivation, and he rarely ends a day without a full yellow page.

Meeting Your Partner's Need

- Take a moment every day to acknowledge your partner for one thing he or she has accomplished. It can be simple, such as, "Darling, great job tidying the garden. It looks terrific." Or, "What a lovely meal, thank you!"

- If your partner is male, at the end of the day, say, "Tell me about your day." Avoid asking, "How was your day?" Men, as a general rule, tend to prefer statements and instructions to questions. Listen for any accomplishments, large or small, that you can acknowledge. When he is finished talking about his day, acknowledge all the accomplishments—for example, "Congratulations for getting that account. You are amazing." He will love this and feel great about you and the relationship. If he felt he didn't accomplish much or is frustrated, remind him how much he has already accomplished or some of his bigger accomplishments in life.

- Help your partner focus on the positive things he or she has achieved, not the few things that didn't get done. Your partner will feel better about himself or herself and will be motivated to carry on. For example, your mate complains that he didn't get time to finish x-y-z project. Tell him that, although he didn't get that done, he did get a-b-c project done instead. Focus on what did get done, even if it seems like a small thing.

- Understand that your partner may be more likely to do things for you as a way of showing his or her love. People with the need to accomplish may work long hours to provide you with a high quality of life. This is often how they show and express their love. Remind your partner that you know this. For example, you could say, "I know you are working hard to provide for me and the family. I really appreciate all that you do for us."

- If you want your partner to spend less time working and more time with you, set it up as a standing appointment in your partner's work calendar or diary. Most people who are good at accomplishing are "get things done" sort of people. If you are on their schedule or calendar it will be more likely to happen. For example, one client had her husband's secretary book in dinner at 7:00 P.M. at home. When her husband saw it in his work calendar, he treated it with just as much professionalism as all his other appointments.

Conversely, if you aren't on his or her schedule, work appointments could easily take over.

- As people with the need to accomplish have a natural tendency to let work take over their personal life, it is important to set up regular structures to maintain romance. One very romantic couple lived in two different cities—one worked in Phoenix and the other in Tucson. Every night they had a standing appointment to call each other and tell each other about their days. And every Friday night, they had a standing appointment at the same cozy little French restaurant where they would meet up to begin their weekend together. Having this simple structure in place made it easy for them to keep their romantic life intact despite living in two different cities. What structures could you put in place that would keep the romance alive in your relationship?

Fred's Story. Fred has three primary needs: to accomplish, to be acknowledged, and the need for order. President of a midsize, rapidly growing company, a confirmed workaholic, divorced three times now, with kids grown, Fred has decided to remain the perennial bachelor as he finds that he can most easily get the appreciation and acknowledgment he needs that way. Once he was married, after a few years the appreciation inevitably turned into criticism and nagging. His need to accomplish drives him to work incredibly hard. He takes his cell phone and computer with him on vacations so that he is never behind on his work.

Fred gets his need for accomplishment met by using a highlighter to mark off what he has done each day. His goal is to get his work done by 3:00 P.M. so he can take the afternoon off to golf. He now works with a handful of clients instead of eighty. Instead of marrying, he prefers to have extended relationships for a number of years. By consciously fulfilling his needs Fred is no longer driven to work countless hours, he has plenty of time to play, and he is light, happy, and free.

3. Appreciated

Acknowledged, Complimented, Esteemed, Flattered, Thanked, Honored, Praised, Prized, Valued, Worthy

You want to know how you are valued and for what reasons. In relationships, you like your partner or spouse to acknowledge and appreciate you for who you are as well as for what you do for him or her. You may bend over backward to do thoughtful things for your partner and will continue to do so as long as you feel he or she appreciates your efforts. You may start to resent your partner or feel that you are being taken for granted if you don't get sufficient appreciation. Like those with the need to be accepted, you also want your boss and colleagues to acknowledge your work, contribution, ideas, projects, and so on. You don't necessarily need a lot of fanfare, but you would like your name mentioned when appropriate, and a few appreciative words can motivate you to work even harder. You may find that you go out of your way to help people, and you enjoy doing so, as long as they give you acknowledgment or praise your efforts. If you don't get the appreciation you want, you might feel taken advantage of and may even get angry, hurt, upset, or resentful. You can prevent this by asking for the credit or acknowledgment you would like beforehand and by gently reminding people to acknowledge you, for example, "How did my comments help you?"

Meeting the Need Through Others

■ Ask five of your closest friends, family members, or colleagues to send a postcard once a week for eight weeks with a message regarding what they appreciate about you and your friendship. If you feel this is too much of an imposition, you may want to stamp and self-address the postcards. One client even wrote the first sentence to get her friends off on the right foot. If they were too busy all they had to do was mail the postcard. If they had a little extra time, they could add a sentence or two of their own. She saved all the cards and put them in a box, and whenever she felt unappreciated, she took out the box and reread some of the cards, which reminded her that she was extremely valued and greatly appreciated.

- Ask five people to call, e-mail, or leave a voice message once a week for the next eight weeks and acknowledge one thing he or she appreciates about you and your friendship. One client asked a friend to do this years ago and they both enjoyed it so much they are still doing it to this day. Experiment with many different requests until you find what works best for you. Don't be afraid to "coach" your friends until they get it just right.

Meeting the Need Yourself

- Tell people in advance how you would like to be appreciated, be thanked, or receive credit for your efforts and contributions, for example, "I'm happy to help you out with this project as long as you put my name on the report as well." Also, gently remind people if they forget to appreciate or thank you: "Tell me what you liked about (the dinner, this project, etc.)."

- Thank people when they appreciate you and accept compliments graciously, for example, "Thank you for noticing. That makes me feel really appreciated."

- Keep a bottle of champagne in the fridge to break open as a reward for a special achievement or occasion as a way to appreciate yourself.

■ Take the time to celebrate the small things you do well every day. Keep a special journal and write down the things you appreciate about your life.

■ Call a family member or friend who is naturally good at appreciating you and share the things you would like to be appreciated for.

Meeting Your Partner's Need

■ Look for opportunities, large and small, to appreciate your partner. For example, you might say, "That lasagna was excellent. You are such a great cook!" The compliment, "Excellent lasagna," is expanded into an acknowledgment, "You are a great cook." If you get in the habit of converting your compliments into acknowledgments, your date will fall in love with you!

■ Ask your partner to tell you how she or he would like to be appreciated and for what, specifically. Does she want you to tell her she is beautiful? Or would she prefer to be valued for her brilliant mind? Or both? You won't know unless you ask your partner.

■ Take a few minutes every day to acknowledge one thing your partner did that you appreciate. This ritual of daily appreciation is easy to start while courting, and then you'll be in the habit to create a lifetime of mutual appreciation for your partner or spouse. How do you get started? "Let's take a few minutes every day to appreciate each other. I'll go first. . . ." Sounds very corny, but it works and feels wonderful.

Margaret's Story. Margaret's partner, John, had the need for appreciation. Every night when they were in bed together, Margaret took a few minutes to share whatever she appreciated

John for that day. Margaret might say, "I really appreciate the wonderful dinner you cooked and that you cleared up afterward so that I'd have time to work on my report. Thanks for your support." And John would acknowledge the appreciation by saying, "Thank you. I appreciate that." Then John would say, "I appreciate that even though you are so busy right now, you took the time to leave me a little sticky note on the fridge. It made me smile." They both enjoyed doing this and the feeling of being appreciated brought them closer together.

4. Clarity

Certainty, Exactness, To Know, Be Informed, Simplicity, Surety

If you have the need for clarity or certainty, you will want to be informed of everything that you feel is relevant or pertinent to the task or situation at hand. In relationships, you will not feel comfortable living with uncertainty. You would need to know what your date or partner expects of you. You like to plan things in advance and probably wouldn't be comfortable traveling without a hotel reservation secured before you left. Some people might think you are being nosy when you are really just keen on being informed. You may read the newspaper or watch the news to stay informed of world events. At work, you like to be kept up-to-date and fully informed. You may not like surprises in any form. You may freely share information, expecting others to do the same only to be disappointed if they don't. You do your best working in an environment that shares information, not for a boss who keeps information to himself or herself.

Meeting the Need Through Others

- Let your friends and family members know that you have a need for clarity and like to be informed. If you are up front about this, then your questions won't seem like such an intrusion or like you are being nosy. You just like to know what is going on in their lives and at work.

- Ask your colleagues and boss to keep you fully informed of events that concern you. You might request a weekly fifteen-minute meeting by phone or in person with your boss to find out what new developments are occurring in the workplace.

- Ladies, avoid asking men too many questions and instead turn your questions into statements. Most men don't like questions and are much more responsive when given an instruction. Try saying, "Tell me about your day." And avoid asking, "How was your day?" For more detail, say, "That's very interesting, please go on."

Meeting the Need Yourself

- Ask for the explanation and clarification that you need. "Could you please clarify?" "Could you expand on that, please?" Or, to avoid too many questions, "Tell me more about that." "Please continue." Or "Do go on."

- Read newspapers and magazines to stay current on events that you are interested in. You can also subscribe to special newsgroups online.

- Join groups or associations that will keep you up-to-date about your professional field.

Meeting Your Partner's Need

- Ask your partner if he or she would feel more comfortable with a prenuptial agreement so that everything is clear up front.

- Some religious sectors have a policy about couples meeting to discuss at length their marital expectations beforehand.

This is an excellent idea for all couples considering marriage and would be particularly beneficial if your potential mate has a need for clarity. If your church doesn't do this, ask a marriage counselor to do it with you as a couple. You *need* to know what to expect.

■ Keep your date or mate well informed. Leave notes and call regularly to keep him or her posted of your whereabouts and activities. Those with a need for clarity don't like being left guessing.

■ Book appointments and dates well in advance.

Rebecca's Story. Rebecca has the need for clarity. She likes to know exactly what is going on. Some people might think she is nosy or a busybody, but she is genuinely interested in what her friends and family are doing. As a result, she is great at staying in contact with letters, phone calls, and e-mails, giving the update on her own life in the hopes of being informed as to what is going on in others' lives. She was driving her husband crazy with her endless questions. After one too many questions, he would get angry and sometimes defensive, even though she didn't mean any sort of criticism. She was simply curious and had to know. Both of them were frustrated as neither of them were getting their needs met.

I asked Rebecca to change one simple thing. She was no longer allowed to ask her husband any questions; instead, she had to use statements. This had miraculous results. Usually, her husband would come home from work and Rebecca would immediately ask the perfectly normal question, "How was your day?" To which he would mutter or grumble, "Fine." Rebecca would ask more specific questions and he would start to get angry and might sulk off to his study to be alone or would turn on the TV to end the interrogation (as he felt it). From her perspective, she was simply being curious and polite. When

Rebecca instead said, "Tell me about your day," while handing him a beverage, he happily recounted the events of the day. She couldn't believe it. Now, she carefully avoids questioning him, knowing that it puts him on the defensive. They are both much happier and their relationship has been completely transformed from mutual annoyance to enjoyment.

5. Control/Power

Administer, Authority, Be in Charge, Command, Conduct, Direct, Dominate, Guide, Govern, Handle, Influence, Lead, Manage, Mastermind, Order, Preside Over, Regulate, Supervise, Superiority, Stamina, Strength

If your need is for power or control, you like to be in charge and very often end up in relationships where your partner prefers to take a backseat. He or she usually lets you call the shots or is very supportive of your goals and career. If you are a woman, then people may remark, "She wears the pants in this relationship." You may be quick to anger, but your anger just as quickly dissipates. You don't tend to hold grudges for long, if at all, since you most often get it out of your system immediately. Others may perceive those with the need to be in control as bossy, curt, or dictatorial. Like those with the need to accomplish, you may tend to put results ahead of people. If you have the need for power or authority you will work hard to obtain a position of leadership or influence. You may or may not need to control others, but you definitely must feel strong and powerful yourself and have the need to influence others to your point of view. Often people with the need for power or influence are executives, politicians, or leaders in charge of people or large responsibilities. Or you may exercise your need for power and control in other ways—being in charge of running the household, children, or community organizations. You may naturally become the matriarch or patriarch of the family. Or you may simply need strength, and if you feel strong, you are content to let others lead the way. Some people need physical strength and stamina in order to feel powerful and have the right emotional makeup to become bodybuilders or marathon runners.

At work, you naturally gravitate to commanding or leadership roles as boss, manager, or supervisor. Or you might own a business so you can be in complete charge. You may become irritated if someone else tries to take control of a meeting or conversation and you reassert your dominance by speaking louder, interrupting, or otherwise attempting to gain control. Although we readily grant men permission to have this need, in the corporate world, controlling, powerful women are often called "bitches." Culturally, we expect women to be softer, more nurturing, and not so controlling or dominating. In truth, both men and women have this need, although women are more reluctant to admit it. You will need the authority commensurate with your responsibilities. Once you feel you have power and control over the areas or domains of your life that are most important to you, you will be willing to let go of the other areas.

Meeting the Need Through Others

- Discuss your need for power or control with your friends and family. Rest assured, they already know about this need, but discussing it will make it easier on them because they will have the chance to grant you control of the domains that are most important to you. For example, one client is a real stickler for the laundry. She is extremely picky about how it should be done and needs complete control over this domain. However, she is happy to let someone else be in charge of the menu planning and grocery shopping. Once you've determined which domains are yours to control, everyone will be much happier.

- Offer to drive, even if it isn't your car. Many people prefer being driven, so this is a handy way to take charge and feel in control.

- Ask your boss to give you the power and authority necessary to get the job done.

- Ask your manager if you can write the agenda for the meetings and check the minutes afterward.

- Ask if you can have the remote control.

Meeting the Need Yourself

- Decide which areas you must control and then delegate the things that really aren't important to you. If you get your need fully met in the areas that are most important to you, you'll find it is easier to let someone else be in control in other areas. For example, you may want to have complete control over the cars, but don't care what happens in the kitchen. Stake out your territory and let everyone involved know.

- Take the time up front to train people properly until they get it right.

- Become the president of a club, group, or organization so you can assert your need to manage others in an appropriate setting.

- You will naturally be drawn to positions of power and authority. Invest in the training you need to get ahead in your career.

- Start and run your own business if you find you can't achieve power working in a company. Or buy a business to run.

- Choose a mate who is happy to let your career take priority over his or hers. You may prefer to marry someone who lets you take charge of the major decisions.

- If you are a bodybuilder or athlete, ask your date or mate to support your activities.

Meeting Your Partner's Need

- Decide together which areas or domains will be under his or her jurisdiction. Write it down and post it on the fridge if needed.

- Be willing to let go of areas that aren't important to you.

- Stick firmly to your own boundaries. If it is your domain, don't let your controlling partner hone in! If your partner tries to tell you how to wash the car, you might gently respond with, "Since when was the car your domain?"

- Let your partner take the lead, such as choosing the restaurant or show. You might ask him or her to order for you in restaurants.

- Know that his or her career might be more important than yours and that your career may not be as important to him or her.

- Support his or her career choices.

Marjorie's Story. Marjorie hated the thought of having a need to be in control. She definitely did not want to have this need. However, she couldn't even let her husband pull out of the driveway without telling him which way to turn. When she started working with me she complained that she had to do everything for her husband and two sons and she was exhausted.

Their marriage was falling apart and she didn't have the energy anymore to maintain it. I asked her why she didn't delegate some of the chores to her eight- and ten-year-old boys—they were certainly old enough to help with the laundry.

"Well, I tried it once and they washed the colors with the whites and all the socks came out pink. Whenever I try to delegate anything, they don't do it right and it just makes more work for me in the end."

The problem was that Marjorie wasn't willing to let go of control. It's no wonder she was exhausted having to manage all the details of her family's life. When she wondered why they couldn't seem to do anything right I pointed out that she had trained them all *not* to do anything, or even think for themselves, so that she could control *everything*. She was training them to be dependent on her. This is how needs can drive us in bizarre ways. Instead of trying not to be so controlling (denying our needs only makes them worse—you have to fulfill a need to make it go away), I asked Marjorie to figure out where she would like to be in control. She said that she would like to be in control of the kitchen, including all meal planning and preparation, the decoration of the home, her own business, and the household budget. I then asked where she would like to relinquish control. Her list included the cars, the computers, the garage, lawn mowing, and household maintenance.

Marjorie sat down with her husband and sons and made a list of all the domains in the household, and as a family they decided who would be the "boss" and responsible for each area. Her older son opted for lawn maintenance and pruning, and her younger son took responsibility for the laundry. Her husband turned over the household finances to her so she could be in control of the overall budget and savings. They agreed to meet monthly to discuss major expenditures together.

Marjorie now had a sense of being in control of things that were important to her, and everyone in the family had his or her own separate domains. At first there was some adjustment; Marjorie had to bite her tongue a few times when she was tempted to control someone else's domain. But they quickly reminded her that this was now their domain. As her need became satisfied, Marjorie noticed that it was easier for her to let go of areas she had tried to control before (such as telling her husband which way to turn out of the driveway). For the first time in years, she was starting to relax and have fun with her family. And her family was taking responsibility for their lives instead of letting Marjorie take care of everything. Now everyone is much happier.

6. Heard/Communicate

Be in Touch, Connected, Convey, Impart, Listened to, Make a Point, Make Contact with, Share Yourself, Tell Stories, Be Understood

This need is fairly common. If you have the need to communicate or be heard, you tend to repeat yourself until you feel heard and the listener acknowledges you. However, when someone repeats himself or herself continually, the listener usually tunes out, which exacerbates the speaker's feeling of not being heard. This happens often in relationships where one person stops listening to the other person. For example, if your partner reads the paper or watches television at the dining table you might not feel heard. Some people have the need to share or tell stories about themselves.

At work, you might fulfill your need to be heard by volunteering to lead the meeting or conducting training courses. You might find a permanent solution by becoming a speaker, trainer, or talk-show host, or finding another appropriate outlet for your wisdom, expertise, or stories. Most people with the need to be heard benefit greatly from installing much bigger boundaries and from finding an appropriate outlet.

Meeting the Need Through Others

- Ask friends, family, or colleagues who are naturally good listeners if they would be willing to listen to you for ten minutes once a week for the next eight weeks. Explain that you don't want coaching or advice. You simply want to be heard. Perhaps ask them at the end to say something like, "Thanks for telling me that," or anything else that would make you feel good.

- Set up a regular monthly phone or online chat with long-distance friends and family members so that you can share your stories and news with them and get an update from them as well.

- At work, if you are speaking with your boss or colleagues and get interrupted, use the four-step model for boundaries and tell them, "Excuse me, but I haven't finished speaking." Or, "Do you mind if I finish my thought first?" Don't let people interrupt you and if they do, make sure you gently remind them by informing them. It is OK to do this in meetings as well; just remember to use a neutral tone of voice.

- Set a time every day to talk to your partner without interruption. This could be a "cocktail" hour after work where you kick back and discuss the day, at dinnertime, or via a phone call if your partner is traveling.

Meeting the Need Yourself

- You might try doing some work, volunteer or otherwise, where you can share your stories and be heard. If you have a therapy issue to resolve, talk it out with a therapist. They are trained listeners. If you have fun stories to share, tell them at parties (just be careful of repeating the same stories to the same people). If you have big goals, then a life coach might be the solution. Most coaches are trained to listen well.

- A permanent solution might be to become a professional speaker and get paid to have people listen to you. This works particularly well if you have a very powerful story and want to keep telling it over and over again. One client lost her twin sons in a car accident. She told the moving and inspiring story of how she dealt with her grief to thousands of people in different audiences.

- Be a guest or host of a radio talk show or teach a class in your community.

- Keep a journal or diary, even if it is just to jot down a few things that happened during the day. It is one way to acknowledge your own thoughts and feelings.

- Meditate every day to give time to hear your own inner thoughts or higher self speak.

- When you call someone, always ask if this is a good time to talk. If not, ask when would be a better time and call later. Don't try to talk when someone is distracted or otherwise busy.

- Acknowledge and thank people who listen to you: "Thank you for listening." Also, if you sense someone has stopped listening, politely ask, "Have you heard this story before?"

Meeting Your Partner's Need

- One of the best things you can say to fulfill your partner's need to be heard might be something like, "Thanks for telling me that," or, "I hear what you are saying," or, "Let me get this straight. You said, (repeat back what you just heard)." If you ignore or fail to acknowledge the speaker, he or she will probably keep repeating the story. If you listen and then try to solve the problem, again, he or she may not feel heard. All you have to do is simply listen—easier said than done for most people.

■ Give your partner ten minutes a day of your complete, undivided attention. Yes, this means you aren't reading the paper or watching TV while your mate is speaking. If your partner knows he or she will have this time, your partner will be less likely to interrupt you while you are doing something else (like watching TV or reading the paper!). After listening to your partner, avoid the temptation to offer advice, come up with a solution, or give coaching.

■ Encourage your partner to find the appropriate forum in which to speak or share stories.

■ Even if you disagree with what your partner says, first respond by saying, "That was a valid point." Or, "That makes sense." Or, "You have a unique perspective. I don't agree with it, but I enjoyed hearing you describe it."

Diane's Story. When Diane complained to me that her boyfriend wasn't listening to her anymore and she feared he was losing interest in the relationship, I guessed that she had the need to be heard or to communicate. Sure enough, this was confirmed when she took the Emotional Index Quiz. She felt she *had* to share her deepest thoughts and feelings and that if her man really loved her, he would want to listen to her. I pointed out that she was expecting one man to meet her need to be heard and communicate when there were countless others who could handily fulfill this role. She agreed to stop trying to share everything with him and instead find a wider audience. She made a list of five of her closest friends and family members and decided to call one each night and share her day's events and thoughts. She discovered that this worked just as well. As long as she had someone to listen to her, she didn't need her boyfriend to fulfill this need. This took the pressure off him and sure enough, he was more interested in hearing what she had to say. When she wanted him to hear her out and not give any advice, she simply said so. This worked really well as he was perfectly content to simply listen. This made it easier for them and he found her more attractive now that she didn't need him so much. Expecting one person to fulfill your needs can put an unnecessary burden on a relationship.

7. Independent

Autonomous, Free, Not Obligated, Self-Sufficient,
Self-Determined, Unattached, Unrestricted

If your need is to be free, independent, or unrestricted, you are self-sufficient, resourceful, and self-motivated. You naturally resist any sort of control, generally do not like being told what to do or how to do things, and may even go so far as to do the opposite of what you are told just to prove that you can't be controlled. You may have a pattern of going out with people who aren't able to commit or aren't truly available (married men or women, someone with significant religious or cultural differences, etc.). If you have this need for freedom, you might find that you shy away from making personal commitments in relationships for fear that it will tie you down or that you'll lose your freedom and independence. This doesn't mean you are destined to be single. If your need for freedom and independence is fulfilled in a variety of ways in and out of the relationship, you can be a loyal and committed partner or spouse. The key is to find ways to fulfill the need so that the relationship doesn't feel constricting or limiting.

In the workplace, you may feel irritated working in a closely managed situation or for a controlling or micromanaging boss. You do best when supervised loosely, if at all. Given full rein, you will come up with your own way of getting the job done thanks to your resourcefulness. You may become an entrepreneur or small-business owner to satisfy the need for independence. This is precisely why you want to work for yourself—you can't stand taking orders from someone else, having to report your actions or activities to someone, or being subservient to another. It is important to get this need fulfilled at work and to find a partner who has his or her needs well fulfilled so that you don't feel the burden of having to take care of another's needs. You may want to manage your own money and have a separate checking account, your own car, or whatever you need to feel free and independent within a committed partnership.

Meeting the Need Through Others

- Tell your manager that you do your best work when given as much freedom as possible. Ask if it would be acceptable for you to report back to him or her on a weekly basis with a progress report. For example, you might say, "I do my best work when I'm not supervised closely. Would a weekly report be sufficient to keep you up-to-date on my progress?" If you take charge of how you'll keep your boss informed, you'll feel more independent in the manager/ employee relationship.

- See if there are jobs in the company that require someone with an entrepreneurial spirit; someone who can take a project and run with it without much supervision.

- Set aside at least one night a week when you have no plans and leave a Saturday or Sunday unscheduled. This gives you time to be spontaneous and do things on a whim. If you are completely booked up, even with fun things, you will probably start to feel boxed in. For example, my hairdresser had the need to not be obligated, and although she had to book in regular appointments for work, she refused to book appointments socially. She said she wanted to be free to decide at the last minute whether to join friends for dinner or to go home and read a good book. Her good friends understood this and were happy to accommodate her request. They simply learned to call her at the last minute and see if she wanted to join them.

- Ask friends and family to only call you before 9:00 P.M. unless it is an emergency.

- Arrange with your partner to have regular free time, saying, for example, "I need time alone every week to do my own thing. I'd like Wednesday nights to be my time. What night would you like for your free evening?"

- Set up a spending plan or budget in which you both have a certain amount of "mad" money each month to spend as you wish.

- Ask for all the time you need to make decisions.

Meeting the Need Yourself

- Take time every day to do what you want. Get up earlier if you have family obligations and go to bed earlier to compensate. One friend gets up at 6:00 A.M. to write her novel an hour before her baby wakes up at 7:00 A.M. and she is off to work at 8:30 A.M. This is her time and she carved it out for herself.

- Learn about money so that you can be financially free. This often makes a huge difference for people who need to be independent. Having enough money so that you don't *have* to work means that work becomes a choice and you are truly free to do it or not. At the very least, save up two years of living expenses. This will be enough so that you can safely say, "Take this job and shove it!" You may never do this, but having the option will fulfill your need for freedom because you won't feel trapped by your job.

- Pay off all your credit cards and other personal debts so you are financially free.

- Put 10 percent a month in a good investment so that you can retire early.

- Own your own car, home, or apartment.

- Choose a romantic partner or spouse who shares the same major life goals so that you are not working at cross-purposes or trying to control each other.

- Tell your partner when you need time alone or time to do your own thing.

- Make sure you have your own checking and savings accounts and do not have to account for your expenditures within an agreed budget.

- Own your own company or business so you can be completely unrestricted. Be wary of getting into business with partners who will want you to account to them. This can be even worse than having a boss if you have the need to be unrestricted.

Meeting Your Partner's Need

- Give your partner all the space and time he or she needs.

- Ask what your partner needs to feel free within a relationship. This may vary tremendously as some couples may agree to open marriages while others simply never get married at all so they can both be free. Be willing to explore all the options, even the radical ones, until you find what works best for you both.

Anna's Story. Anna used to go out with men who were great at cherishing her but really weren't available for marriage for one reason or another. Some would say she had a "fear of commitment," but it wasn't commitment that she feared. It was losing her freedom and independence. When Anna took the plunge and married, she realized that there can be freedom and independence within a commitment. She was surprised that she felt freer once she was married thanks to the support of her husband in a myriad of ways. Instead of taking care of everything herself, she could rely on him to handle the cars and car insurance, to take care of maintenance issues around the house, and best of all, he loved to cook and do the shopping. This freed Anna to focus on her legal career and other things that were important to her. He also encouraged her to do what she needed to do to get ahead in her career. If she needed to work late, that wasn't a problem. The support and love she felt from her husband gave her more time to do what she wanted in her life. Anna also has regular nights out to take classes she is interested in and spend time with her girlfriends. Her partner respects her need for freedom and gives her the time and space to do things independently.

8. Integrity/Honesty

Authenticity, Genuine, Forthright, Factual, Loyalty, Openness, Sincerity, Truthful

Everyone has this need to varying degrees. Honesty and integrity are the foundation of every successful relationship. But what constitutes honesty and integrity for one person wouldn't for another. For example, while one client wouldn't think of taking a single postage stamp or paper clip from her employer, another thinks nothing of popping her personal mail in the office post. Is she a devious criminal, a horrible person, and untrustworthy?

Not at all. She is a loving and generous person, but she feels there is nothing wrong with using the company's post office. These are two different levels of honesty and integrity. Bonnie and Clyde were great partners, but partners in crime. While I personally wouldn't want an open marriage, it works for some couples as long as they are honest about it. The level of honesty and integrity that you require in a relationship will very much depend on your own personal level. If this comes up as one of your needs, you probably have a higher level of honesty and integrity than most people and would find it difficult to be in a relationship with someone with lower standards. And, you wouldn't feel comfortable working for someone you consider to have little or no integrity. You will not tolerate being lied to in any case.

Meeting the Need Through Others

- Tell your family and friends that you have the need for honesty and that you would prefer to know the truth, even if it is hard to hear. Ask them to clear the air and reveal any secrets they might have been keeping from you.

- At work, if you catch someone in a lie, confront him or her privately and let the person know it is not acceptable to be dishonest with you in any form.

- Tell your date or mate that you prefer complete honesty and openness in a relationship.

Meeting the Need Yourself

- Maintain firm and clear boundaries around your need for honesty and integrity. Use the four step communication model to inform people when you feel they are out of line.

- Surround yourself with honest people by working for a good company with a solid reputation and integrity.

- If you feel uncomfortable with someone's level of integrity, then let that person know. If he or she doesn't change, then it is best to move on and find someone who is on the same level.

Meeting Your Partner's Need

- It is best to be completely honest and forthright with your partner. Be yourself. Do not pretend to be someone other than who you are. He or she will prefer that you are honest from the beginning and that will engender more trust than trying to impress someone by exaggerating your circumstances or making false claims.

- Tell the whole truth, not just the partial truth. Your partner will respect you more.

- Raise your own level of integrity to match your partner's. If he or she is adamant about following rules and common courtesies, then do the same. If your partner doesn't speed, then stick to the limit. Consider it a growth opportunity.

Larry and Stephanie's Story. Larry has the need for honesty, integrity, and loyalty. He cannot stand being with someone who lies or cheats, and he knows that he could never be in a relationship with a woman who wasn't faithful and loyal to him. Larry was happily married to Stephanie and they had a stable marriage. Everything was fine until Larry had an extramarital affair with a woman he met at work. On the advice of his friends, he didn't tell Stephanie for fear that it would hurt her and that she would leave him. But he couldn't bear keeping this deceit between them and decided to end the affair and come clean and confess to his wife that he had the affair and that it was over. Honesty was the only way to save the integrity of their marriage. Stephanie was terribly hurt and extremely angry and asked him to move out of the house for some time.

After a few months, she decided that it was more important that he had been honest with her and she preferred that to him hiding the affair from her. She decided to forgive him and take him back. After a few difficult months, they are doing fine now because Stephanie knows she can trust Larry to be honest with her even when it isn't easy to do so.

9. Loved/Cherished

Adored, Admired, Desired, Liked, Held Fondly, Preferred, Relished, Treasured

This is such a common need for most singletons that I've given it extra attention in this chapter. If this is one of your needs, welcome to the crowd. You are a very loving, caring, and sensitive person. You might not have had enough loving and cherishing as a child or even if you had loving parents, you just need more loving, holding, or cherishing than others. Oddly enough, you may subconsciously choose relationships where you aren't getting enough love and may be perceived as "clingy" or "needy." Or you might have the tendency to stay in relationships too long, thinking that the problem lies with you and that, if you try a bit harder, you will figure out how to make it work. The signs that the relationship is one-sided may be obvious to your friends and family, but you may persist until it becomes painfully obvious that your partner isn't willing or able to love you fully or commit to a loving partnership.

To get this need fulfilled, you probably focus on your romantic and love relationships and expect your partner to fulfill all your needs. The mistake is thinking that your partner is the only one who can and should fill your need to be loved or cherished. In fact, friends and family can do this brilliantly and take the pressure off the relationship, which, ironically, tends to bring back the original feelings of love.

You might also be trying to fulfill your need to be loved or cherished by overeating comforting foods or overspending. The momentary high is a temporary way of feeling good. Unfortunately, no amount of shoes, clothes, cosmetics, or chocolate donuts can truly fulfill the need to be loved or cherished. If you are hiding your snacks or your purchases, there is most definitely an unmet need lurking about, driving this behavior. Most people find that when their need to be loved is fulfilled in healthy ways, their compulsion to shop or eat tends to disappear naturally.

There are many healthy ways to fulfill the need to be loved or cherished. But not all things work for all people. While one person might feel cherished by close physical contact such as holding hands in public, another might be embarrassed or uncomfortable showing public displays of affection. Pick from the suggestions later in the chapter to determine what will work best for you, and add your own as you discover them. But take note: it really makes it easier on the person cherishing and adoring you if you tell him or her specifically what you want or need.

If you have the need to be loved or cherished, it is highly likely that you have inadequate or missing boundaries. It is very hard to feel loved if you allow your boss or clients to yell at you or if friends, family, and colleagues are giving you unsolicited criticism. Even snide comments or jests meant in fun can make you feel bad. It is like trying to fill a bucket with water when the bucket has a big hole in the bottom. No matter how much loving and cherishing you have coming in, it is never enough if you don't have strong boundaries in place. Your need has little or no chance of being fulfilled because you are putting yourself in a situation that constantly creates more neediness. You are, in effect, allowing people to poke holes in your bucket. Patch the holes with strong boundaries and *bingo*, just a drop of water (loving and cherishing) coming in at the top and your bucket is very quickly filled and soon overflowing. Because so many people who have this need have weak or nonexistent boundaries, I've included a list of key boundaries that you may want to add to your own list.

Boundaries

- No one may yell at me.
- No one may give me unsolicited advice or criticism.
- No one may take advantage of me.
- No one may make rude, put-down comments or jokes about me.
- No one may argue in my presence.

Meeting the Need Through Others

- If you are reading this book, in all probability, this is one of your biggest needs. If you have the need to be loved or cherished, you are probably relying too much on your partner to meet it. With many of the other needs, it is fine to ask your partner, but I'd recommend a different tactic for this particular need. Postpone asking your romantic partner to fulfill this need until you've asked at least five other people to meet it first. Make it as easy as possible by asking people who already love you, but whatever you do, *do not skip this step!* If you have this need, it is especially important that you ask others to meet it. You cannot, I repeat, you *cannot* get this particular need met all by yourself. It is very much like giving yourself a massage. It doesn't feel the same at all and isn't nearly as satisfying. You can be creative in how you ask for this need to be fulfilled. But first, think carefully about what will make you feel loved, and then be *very specific* in your requests.

- Ask your loved ones to send you any of the following: note cards, postcards, e-mails, phone calls with cherishing words and thoughts, small gifts or flowers—whatever fulfills your need to be loved, but again, remember to be very specific in your requests. The more specific the request, the easier it is to satisfy. One client had the need to be cherished, but she also had the need to be surprised. She didn't want to know in advance what any one person would do to cherish her. She made a list of all the things that made her feel cherished and gave it to five people. They could then pick anything from the list and do it for her, once a week for the next eight weeks. This way she had her need fulfilled and was surprised by each gift, card, or phone call.

- Create a "box of love," which sits next to the entrance of either your house or, if appropriate, your office. Next to it place little slips of paper. Upon entering your house, your guests are asked to write you a small love/cherish note and deposit it into the box. At the end of each week, you can sit down and read through the notes from your "box of love"!

- Send your friends and family a pack of eight postcards, pre-stamped and addressed, and ask them to write you a cherishing or loving note and drop it in the mail once a week for the next eight weeks.

- Ask your significant other to call you every day around lunchtime while you are at work, just to say, "I love you."

- Ask your manager and colleagues at work to tell you what they see are your greatest strengths and what they like about working with you.

Meeting the Need Yourself

- Stop all negative self-talk the moment you notice it. Just say silently, "Cancel, cancel."

- Every morning and evening write in a journal what you cherish about yourself and the ways others have shown they love you.

- Take a hot bubble bath.

- Buy fresh flowers to brighten your home and office or invest in very good quality silk flowers that look like the real ones.

- Hire a chef or have a service deliver home-cooked meals to your door. One client decided that instead of a weekly session with a personal trainer at the gym, she would rather have a personal chef come to her home once a month to prepare healthy meals that she could freeze and reheat throughout the month. Make sure you are doing what really makes *you* feel loved, not what you think you *should* do.

- When you wake up in the morning and look in the bathroom mirror, smile and say, "Good morning, gorgeous!"

- Choose relationships with those who are willing and able to love you back.

- Acknowledge others when their actions make you feel loved.

- Learn to accept and receive compliments and gifts graciously (as opposed to rebuffing them with comments such as, "You shouldn't have." Or "What, this old thing?").

- Inform people immediately if they cross any of your boundaries. If you realize after the fact that a boundary has been crossed, inform them as soon as possible afterward.

- Take extremely good care of yourself (personal trainer, life coach, nutritionist, weekly massage, facials, housekeeper, etc.). This reinforces that you are worthy and deserving of special care and attention. Since like attracts like, the better you take care of yourself, the better others will take care of you as well. Cherish yourself and you'll attract people who cherish you.

- Get a dog that adores you!

- Sign up for a book-of-the-month club to give yourself a gift each month for one of your hobbies or interests. You might choose a cookbook club, a decorating book club, or any of a number of other specialty groups. As a less expensive alternative, get a magazine subscription for a monthly treat.

- Sign up for a flower club and receive a beautiful, potted seasonal flower to brighten up your home—another gift that keeps on giving throughout the year.

How Your Partner Can Meet Your Need

- Now that you've asked your friends and family to meet your need, you can ask your romantic partner as well. Keep in mind that men respond particularly well to specific requests. The owner of a flower shop shared her story in one of my Irresistible Attraction seminars. She had just had a huge argument with her husband. He screwed up on something (and it must have been a pretty big something) and he said, quite sincerely, "I'm terribly sorry." She replied, "That isn't good enough. What you did demands a seven-dozen-red-roses apology!" Although she never meant him to take her literally, the next day he came home bearing seven dozen red roses. She burst out laughing and after that she couldn't possibly be mad at him and completely forgave him. If you want something specific, ask.

- Ask your partner to massage your neck, shoulders, or feet whenever appropriate.

- Ask your partner to bring you your favorite flowers every week.

- The more you show your appreciation for the loving gestures or comments your date makes, the more you will receive.

- If you like loving notes left in surprise locations, hand your partner a sticky note pad and write the first few to get him or her started on the right track.

- Set up a regular weekly date night and take turns planning romantic candlelit evenings out for each other (you can do this at home if you prefer). Get dressed up; wear sexy underwear. Go on dates just like when you first met. Have your date open the car door, pay for dinner, the works. If you wonder where the romance has gone, then this is probably the missing bit.

- Ask your partner to bring your coffee or tea to you while you are still in bed.

- Tell your partner how to please you in bed.

- Reinforce the comments that make you feel good. For example, say things like, "I love it when you tell me how beautiful I am."

- Instead of asking, "How do I look?" Try, "Tell me I'm gorgeous!" Or, let your partner know that when you ask, "How do I look?" the appropriate response is, "Absolutely beautiful!" Or similar. (Most have already figured this one out, but some need training.)

- Ask to be held tenderly or cuddled.

- Ask your partner to softly stroke your hair.

Meeting Your Partner's Need

- Simply ask your partner what makes him or her feel loved, cherished, and adored. Don't let your partner get away with some vague, general answer such as "I know that you love me" or "The little things." Press for specifics. Is it that you make tea or coffee in the morning just the way your partner likes it? Is it that you open doors and act chivalrously? Is it love notes left around the house? Gifts? Cards? Caring words? Or, does your partner prefer loving gestures such as holding hands or playing footsies under the table?

- Ask your partner to make a specific list of the things that make him or her feel loved and keep the list handy for your own reference. Add to the list as you discover more things about your partner's needs. Get in the habit of doing one thing a day to fulfill your romantic partner's need to be loved and cherished and you'll be amazed at the results.

- If you are being taken out on a date, never critique the meal or show. Just point out the positive aspects of the experience. It took me years to realize that women bond by sharing both positives and negatives of an experience, but if a man is taking you out, stick to the positive. It is just the same as if he actually cooked the dinner himself or acted in the show. He'll feel bad if you aren't enjoying it. So find the one positive thing and comment on that. Men respond very well to gracious expressions of love.

■ Every night before bed, tell your partner how much you love him or her. Make it a ritual.

Sandra's Story. As soon as Sandra, a successful judge and divorced mother of two, discovered her top needs, she wasted no time in telling the charming man she was dating that she needed to be treasured. He immediately picked up the hint and started showering her with gifts that included jewelry, boxes of high-quality chocolates, and gorgeous floral bouquets. She told me all this was very nice, but to her, being treasured meant that he would whisper sweet nothings in her ear and give her hand a secret squeeze. She didn't want "stuff." She wanted affectionate actions.

I asked her if she had been specific with her boyfriend when she told him she liked to be treasured. Sandra sheepishly admitted that she hadn't. All she had told him was that she needed to be treasured. After thanking him for the many lovely presents, she told him that what she really wanted was affectionate gestures and gave him a few examples of things she liked. He was more than happy to comply with her request.

Remember, if you aren't specific, you might find yourself feeling disappointed even though you know intellectually you shouldn't be. This man could have continued to shower Sandra with chocolates and gifts and she never would have felt truly satisfied. This is a perfect example of why you need to be very specific when you tell your partner or spouse what you want.

10. Luxury

Abundance, Comfort, Coziness, Ease, Indulgence, Prosperity, Relaxed, Restful

One client jokingly remarked that if she is staying at a hotel and there is no chocolate on the pillow, she feels like she is "roughing it." She certainly has the need for luxury or indulgence. As someone with the need for comfort, you might want a home that has plenty of easy chairs and comfortable beds and probably a well-stocked fridge and larder. If you need luxury, comfort, or abundance you don't want to feel like you are struggling, uncomfortable, or deprived in any way. Another client said she thought the ultimate luxury would be to have freshly cleaned and ironed sheets on her bed every night in order to really feel at home.

You may also want to be with someone who enjoys the finer things in life as well, such as gourmet food as opposed to fast food, three-hundred-thread-count sheets instead of poly-cotton blends, and goose down pillows instead of foam. In relationships, you will do best with someone who doesn't find your need for luxury to be wasteful or frivolous. It is important that your romantic partner appreciate and respect your need instead of mocking it.

It is also important to make your work environment as luxurious and comfortable as possible. Request an ergonomic chair and work station, use a headset if you talk on the phone, and make sure you have everything you need at hand. Bring in fresh flowers for your desk and see if you can hang artwork on the walls to make your office or cubicle as luxurious and comfortable as possible.

Many people may want luxury in their lives, but won't be negatively affected if they don't have it. However, if you need luxury, it is a requirement for you to feel your best, and without it, you may even become depressed.

Meeting the Need Through Others

- If you are going out for a meal, suggest a few restaurants that you know to be excellent and affordable. If your need is for luxury, you may prefer to go out once a month to a really fine restaurant. If your need is for abundance, you might prefer to go out weekly to a more affordable place.

- Let your boss know what your requirements are if you travel for business often. Travel in business class and make sure your hotel has good accommodations such as a gym or spa or a massage to help you relax upon arrival.

- Ask your date or mate for whatever you feel you need. Let him or her know whether you prefer quantity over quality or quality over quantity. Do you want one perfect rose or a massive bunch of daisies? He or she has no way of knowing unless you say.

- Make gift giving easy by letting your friends and family know what you like or by registering at a favorite shop. Make sure that there are affordable items on your list so as not to put anyone under financial pressure.

Meeting the Need Yourself

- Sleep on three-hundred-thread-count or better sheets and use the best quality mattress you can afford. Use 100 percent goose down pillows.

- Add luxury to your life in little ways, such as tossing fresh raspberries into your morning bowl of Cheerios, grinding your own coffee or buying an espresso machine to make great coffee at home, using special hand soap, and using your favorite brands of products throughout the house.

- Make sure your chair is perfectly comfortable.

- Hire a housekeeper, gardener, and as much domestic help as you can afford. At the very least, though, have a housekeeper clean the whole house or apartment once a month and gradually add more time as you can afford it.

- Grow your own flowers or herbs in a pot so you always have them on hand.

- Get a regular manicure, pedicure, massage, or whatever makes you feel pampered, luxurious, or spoiled.

- Travel with your own pillow.

Meeting Your Partner's Need

- Ask your romantic partner what his or her favorites are—flowers, restaurants, chocolates, and so forth. Some people like roses and others prefer tulips. Some like dark chocolate and some like milk. You'll never know unless you ask.

- If traveling, remember to pack your partner's pillow.

- Ask your date or mate, "What would make you feel more comfortable?" Or, "How can I make you feel more comfortable?"

- Understand that this is a real need for your partner. He or she isn't being silly or frivolous. People with this need simply aren't their best if they don't feel comfortable. While you might be comfortable sleeping on poly-cotton sheets, your partner might find them scratchy or too hot and not get a good night's sleep.

- Give your date or mate gift certificates for spa and beauty treatments.

- Go to restaurants where both the service and the food is excellent.

Sarah's Story. Sarah has the need for abundance, luxury, and comfort. She travels with her own pillow, has a special scented hand soap in her desk at work that she takes with her when she goes to the restroom, uses an ergonomic keyboard and chair at the office, and sleeps on the finest quality sheets she can find and the best mattress. She loves her comfort and luxury. She was perfectly happy fulfilling her own need and didn't even notice it was a need (since fulfilled needs "disappear") until she got into a relationship with William, a very kind, practical, hardworking, highly principled man who believes charity to others comes first. Suddenly her need for luxury became a problem. He couldn't see or appreciate the difference and felt that luxuries were fine as the occasional gift or present, but that really such indulgences were unnecessary, superfluous, and frivolous.

Being a sensitive person who also wanted to help others, Sarah agreed and stopped buying luxuries so they could save their money. Unfortunately, this made her feel deprived, so she'd go out on occasion on a spending spree and hide her purchases from William, knowing he disapproved of them. She even kept a separate credit card in secret and had racked up thousands of dollars in debt without telling him. This was unhealthy, creating a hidden tension between them.

I asked Sarah to come clean about her spending and her credit card with her husband. Naturally, she was afraid to do this, knowing he would blow up. I said it was better that he realize she was hiding the debt than that he think she was having an affair, and she decided to tell him. I also suggested that they allow a set sum each month, say a hundred dollars each, for "mad" money. This money could be used to buy whatever they wanted, and as long as she stayed within the agreed budget, she could do whatever she wanted without any fear of criticism or comment from William. He in turn could spend his money however he chose. He could save it for a rainy day, donate it to charity, or buy something he wanted.

Armed with this strategy, Sarah felt brave enough to approach William with the truth. Sure enough, he was furious, not so much about the debt but that Sarah hid it from him. She explained that she was hiding the debt because she knew he wouldn't approve of her purchases and suggested they set aside some monthly "mad" money. He agreed to try it out and they both found it worked beautifully. Sarah no longer had to hide her purchases and he no longer criticized her. Sarah reported back to me that understanding her needs has saved their relationship.

11. Order

Checklists, Cleanliness, Discipline, Neatness, Organization, Perfection, Plans, Regularity, Routines, Structure, Tidiness

There are actually two types of people when it comes to order. Some are organized internally and can function in an externally disorganized space. Other people are organized externally and require an ordered physical environment to think clearly. Remember, our needs are requirements for us to be our best. If you have the need for order, it simply isn't an option for you to live or work in a messy environment. If you do, you will always feel frustrated. On the other hand, if you happen to *like* order but can function well in a messy environment, then order is not one of your top needs.

If you live with a messy person, you might have to set separate rooms aside in the house where your partner can be messy and you can shut the door on the space. For shared spaces, you will need a tidy, ordered environment or you won't feel comfortable or be able to relax. At work, you would be miserable sharing a cubicle with a messy person, so request to share spaces with one of the tidier employees. Fortunately, most people with the need for order are naturally tidy and fulfill this need themselves automatically and instinctively.

Meeting the Need Through Others

- Let your friends, family, and loved ones know that you have a need for order and you simply can't think clearly or relax in a disordered space. It isn't that you are trying to be picky or difficult.

- Ask your roommate or partner to keep the shared spaces tidy. Make sure your mate has at least one separate room of his or her own to keep the clutter and messiness contained.

- Make sure everything in your home has a designated place so that it is easy for others to maintain the order you have established.

- Give your housekeeper a checklist for each room to ensure it is maintained the way you like it.

Meeting the Need Yourself

- Hire a housekeeper who keeps things orderly and teach your loved ones how to put things away properly.

- Hire a professional organizer to put the entire house in order and create easy-to-maintain systems. A good system makes it hard for packrats to make messes because the system is easier to use than their own method; therefore, they will be more likely to use it than not and everyone will be happy.

- Create checklists to organize your life and keep copies of these lists on hand.

- One executive who traveled frequently kept a duplicate set of all her cosmetics and shampoos in a travel bag so that she didn't have to unpack it after each trip.

- Set up systems and organize things so that less organized people know where items belong (labels on drawers, files, etc.).

- Make sure you have your own side of the closet and your own dresser or drawers for clothing.

Meeting Your Partner's Need

- Set up the appropriate domains. For example, if your partner does most of the cooking and meal preparation, then it makes sense that the kitchen is his domain and he should be allowed to put the utensils in the drawers that make the most sense to him. You need to respect that this is primarily his domain and keep it tidy, putting things back in the original places.

- Have a separate room of your own, such as a study or an office, so that you are able to organize yourself without having to share a space. But if you must share spaces, clearly designate which part of the space is yours and which part of the space is your partner's. If you are a packrat you'll have to work harder to keep things neat. Remember, your partner isn't trying to be fussy. He or she simply can't function well in a disorganized space.

- If you are living with someone who is neat as a pin and you are prone to collect things or have cluttered living spaces, hire a professional organizer. The messiest of people can learn how to be tidier. They often just lack the systems needed to keep things organized and once they have the system, they are fine. (An example of such a system is a "California-style" closet where there is a specifically designed space for everything.)

- Get in the habit of tidying a room before you leave it so that when you return, it always looks nice.

Paula's Story. Paula has the need for order and lives with her boyfriend who is a bit on the sloppy side. When she comes home after a hard day's work and opens the door to her apartment to find the bed unmade, towels on the bathroom floor, and clothes lying outside the hamper, she can't help but feel irritable. Because her need for order is not being met, she feels angry, resentful, or crabby when she speaks to her boyfriend. Or, she might tidy things up and not say a thing to him, hoping that one day he'll learn from her example. Eventually, Paula blows up and yells at her boyfriend, calling him a slob. He'd make an effort to be tidier, but eventually, his old habits would return and the same scenario would repeat itself.

Paula realized that her boyfriend, Jim, didn't have any space to be messy. He didn't have a room of his own in the apartment for his own things and his "clutter." They agreed that he could have the second bedroom for his collections. In shared spaces, Paula set about creating a specific space for everything, even going so far as to label the drawers. Once there was a place for everything, Jim found it much easier to know where to put things and was able to keep the common spaces neat and tidy without a lot of effort. Paula didn't blow up anymore and their relationship soon improved to the point where Jim asked her to marry him!

It always works best for a relationship if the need for order prevails, so the packrat must respect this need if it is going to work in the long run, but the person with the need for order should make it easy for the other person. Professional organizers can really save the day in these relationships, so it is well worth the initial expense and will save countless arguments down the road.

12. Peace/Balance

Agreements, Be Alone, Calmness, Harmony, Reconciliation, Serenity, Silence, Tranquility, Quiet

If peace or balance is one of your needs, you may find that you feel out of sorts all day if you miss your morning meditation, your walk with the dog, or your journaling time. In relationships, you might find that you avoid conflict and will go to great lengths to appease your partner and keep the peace. You may be the family peacemaker and find yourself mediating conflicts because you value harmony. Or, you might find that you retreat or run away from arguments or conflicts. At work, people with the need for peace and stillness may find it impossible to do their best work in a chaotic or loud environment. If balance is your need, define what sort of balance you need. This can be work and play, social time and alone time, traveling and staying at home. Balance is one of my needs, and I definitely strive to live a balanced life—after yoga class, I go right out and have a beer and a hamburger! Balance is a need you can usually meet by yourself, but you can also ask people to help you. There is much talk these days about living a balanced life, but if this isn't one of your needs, don't sweat it. Focus on your own needs, not on everyone else's. Some people need balance and some don't.

Meeting the Need Through Others

- While the need for peace and harmony is one that you can usually fulfill yourself, don't be afraid to ask other people to help you with it. For example, one busy executive told her massage therapist to call her if she neglected to schedule an appointment. She knew that if she was too busy to make the appointment, then she *definitely* needed the massage!

- Tell people specifically how they can support your need. For example, you might ask your partner, "Please make dinner so I can meditate for half an hour."

- Set boundaries around your personal time. Make sure no one interrupts you during your quiet time (bath, writing, meditation).

Meeting the Need Yourself

- Try this simple exercise. Every day, for at least ten minutes, sit in a quiet place and do nothing. Just be quiet and peaceful. I have one client who sits in the supply closet at work. The supply closet is the only place no one would think to look for him at work. Just ten minutes a day gives him an amazing sense of peace.

- Do whatever it takes to carve out personal time. My clients report that without some sort of quiet time they run around like crazy, but don't seem to accomplish much. Learn to meditate. Take a yoga class. Focus on your breathing. Lock the door and take a bath.

- Do something every day to create a sense of peace and stillness. Write in a journal every morning or evening to clear your brain. One client finds that ironing gives her peace.

- Take time to nurture yourself every week, especially if under stress (a weekly massage, yoga, manicure, facial, etc.).

- Live and work in a peaceful neighborhood or office. Consider a move from the city to the country in order to meet the need for peace and harmony. Or, if you must work in a city, request flex time and work four days a week in the city and spend three days in the country.

- Walk or bike to work instead of driving to help you relax and feel peaceful before you arrive at work and before you return home.

- Spend time in nature; it is a natural stress reducer. If you live in a city, make sure to spend time in nature on weekends or try to have lunch in a local park.

- Use voice mail instead of answering the phone, or turn the phone off.

- Downsize and live a simpler life so you can work part-time and have more time for yourself.

Meeting Your Partner's Need

- Be willing to move to a quieter neighborhood if you live in a noisy or congested area.

- Accompany your partner for a walk in the park or on the beach. Take this time to enjoy the quiet and peaceful quality of nature. At the same time, this lets your partner know that you are willing to support his or her need.

- Understand that your partner needs quiet time every day in order to function at his or her best. Support your partner by setting aside this time.

- Do not dismiss your partner's need as silly or unimportant. While you may not need half an hour a day of peace, it makes all the difference to your partner.

Katherine's Story. Katherine, a journalist, was becoming increasingly stressed in her new office. The management team decided to make it an open floor plan so that communication and ideas could flow. Unfortunately for Katherine, she couldn't string two thoughts together with all the noise and interruptions. Her work was suffering and she was incredibly stressed. She came home in the evenings with a headache and complained to her boyfriend, but then she was so worried, she wasn't sleeping well. This made her irritable and crabby. Her boyfriend started talking about moving out.

She called me desperately afraid she was losing both her job and her man. I told her it was simply a case of an unfulfilled need. She needed peace. I encouraged her to talk to her boss about getting time away from the fray to write. He denied her request because there was no way to give her a private office and not the others. She could, however, choose to work off-site. In the end, she discovered she was fine if she could hang out with her laptop at a quiet coffee shop. Her work and productivity improved immediately, her stress levels dropped, and she no longer feared she'd lose her job. On the personal front, she no longer came home complaining and her original enthusiasm for her writing returned. She was able to sleep through the night and her boyfriend decided to stick around to see how the relationship would develop over time.

13. Recognized

Acclaimed, Admired, Applauded, Be Seen, Celebrated, Cheered, Commended, Get Credit, Glorified, Honored, Known, Noticed

If you need recognition, you might go out of your way to get it by working harder than your colleagues, by getting credentialed so that you are recognized as a leader in your field or industry, by working on high-profile projects, and by doing things to be known, seen, or noticed. Socially, you might clown around to get attention, tell jokes, or play practical jokes. If you won any trophies, prizes, awards, or certificates you'll have them prominently displayed in your home or office, not hidden away in a box in the attic. You will work hard to achieve recognition. You might wear something different so that you'll stand out from the crowd. You want to be seen, to be known, to be somebody. In relationships, you look to your partner to give you attention. You need him or her to recognize your accomplishments and abilities. When you have this, you are much more confident and self-assured and can achieve great things.

Meeting the Need Through Others

- Ask five family members, friends, or colleagues to call, e-mail, or write to you with one thing they admire about you once a week for the next eight weeks. You might ask them to share what they are proud of you for, what they see as your most significant accomplishments, or what your unique talents or gifts are. If there is something specific that you'd like recognition for, ask for that as well. You could ask them to tell you what they notice about you or in what ways they respect you. For example, you might say, "Tell me what you see as my contribution to this family or team."

- Ask to be introduced if you are at a party or event and do not know everyone. Tell the host how you'd like to be introduced if you'd like to be known for something, for example, "Please introduce me as Dr. Johnson, the author of (fill in the blank)" or "the owner of XYZ business."

- Tell your boss that you are motivated by recognition and how you would like to be recognized and rewarded for your efforts. If you want the title and have earned it, ask for it.

- Request the title and salary increase that goes with an increase in responsibility and authority at work.

- Tell your partner what you'd like to be recognized for specifically.

- Ask your friends or family members to throw a birthday party in your honor.

Meeting the Need Yourself

- Join groups or associations where you can be recognized for your participation.

- Volunteer at a well-respected charity or organization where they recognize their supporters.

- Surround yourself with your awards and certificates to remind yourself of your successes.

- Attend social events and parties where people know you.

- Join a golf club or other club where you can get to know people.

- Write a monthly column for a magazine or newspaper so that you are a recognized authority.

- Become a master in your field. Get known as the expert on any topic that interests you.

- Run a marathon so you can get cheered on by all the bystanders.

- Learn to play one great piece on the piano so you can play at others' houses or parties and soak up the applause.

Meeting Your Partner's Need

- Ask your date or mate what you can do or say specifically to meet his or her need. Would your partner like you to say something, write it in a card or letter, or hold a party in his or her honor?

- Listen to your partner and acknowledge him or her for any achievements, however, small.

- Hang your mate's successes on the wall. Frame important documents or certificates and give trophies and awards a place of honor in your home.

- Give your partner a plaque, certificate, or engraved trophy such as Husband of the Year or Best Mother on the Planet or World's Best Lover. If they have the need, even if they think it is silly, they will secretly still love it.

- Make a big deal of your partner's birthdays. It should be a special occasion with all the works. Make sure he or she is the center of attention. Invite friends around to join in the celebration.

- If your mate or date gets a promotion or other achievement, hold a party with friends and colleagues and make an announcement about his or her success. Go around the room and ask each person to give an acknowledgment as well.

Daniel's Story. Daniel had the need to be seen. He so desperately wanted to be recognized that he would regularly stop at restaurants on his way home from work to see if anyone he knew was dining there. If he saw people he knew, he'd go over to their table and say hello and chat for a few minutes and then drive on to the next restaurant. He was a very successful businessman, had been married, had two grown kids, and was now divorced and looking for the ideal woman.

After a few calls, it became clear that Daniel needed to be recognized by his father. His father had criticized him all his life. He wanted his father to approve of him and tell him he thought he had done well with his life. I asked Daniel to call his father and ask him to tell him what he thought he had done well in life. Daniel did not want to do this. Week after week he resisted the assignment with one excuse after another until finally, he asked his father to write him a letter, which his father agreed to do. The letter listed all of Daniel's accomplishments, and he wrote how proud he was to have such a son. This fulfilled Dan's need so completely that he found he stopped going into restaurants looking for recognition. He now had what he felt had always been missing—his father's love, approval, and recognition. With his needs fulfilled, he stopped wasting time looking for recognition, joined a golf club to play and relax more, and met a very bright, talented, and sexy woman on the putting green. They have been happily seeing each other ever since.

Sometimes things don't always work out so neatly. I had one client who wanted to be recognized by his father, but his father had died a few years earlier. He wasn't sure exactly what his father thought of him. I asked him to talk to his mother and other relatives to find out what things his father had said about him that he may not have told his son. Another technique is to write a letter to the deceased person and write back the letter you think he or she would have written.

Finally, you may have to admit that not everyone is willing or able to fulfill your needs. Lucinda, a busy and very successful advertising executive, needed recognition from her mother. Lucinda liked to receive thoughtful, handmade gifts, and she asked her mother to give her a special, handmade card or gift once a week for the next eight weeks to fulfill her need to be recognized. The first week she didn't receive anything, so I told her to gently remind her mother. Her mother replied that she didn't know what to make. Lucinda told her that a single rose from her lovely garden would be perfect. And to her delight, her mother made her a beautiful bouquet of flowers picked by hand from her garden. The next week, her mother didn't do anything. Lucinda was devastated. It became clear that her mother was very needy herself and that she didn't have the capacity to meet her daughter's needs.

It was time for Lucinda to look for someone else to fulfill her needs. This wasn't easy for Lucinda to admit. It is natural that we want our parents to fulfill our needs, but sometimes our parents simply can't. They may have too many issues of their own to contend with. In this case, find a surrogate to do the job. It might be another relative, loving in-laws, or good friends you ask instead. The good news is that while it is nice to have our parents fulfill our needs, other people can fulfill them just as effectively. So you are not off the hook! Keep asking until you really feel satisfied.

14. Responsible

Accountable, Commitments, Devoted, Duty, Do the Right Thing, Justice, Loyalty, Have a Mission or Cause, Obliged, Pledge

If you have a need for duty, you may feel compelled to do the right thing. You may satisfy others even at the expense of your own health and well-being, feeling obligated to put family, friends, or work ahead of yourself even to the point of risking your health or life. You might have a need to be a devotee and follow a leader or an important cause. You might be a missionary or social worker willing to work for very little money and put your life at risk in order to help other people. Or you might feel compelled to prove yourself regardless of the personal costs. At work, you may work long hours because you feel a strong sense of duty to your work and feel obligated to do whatever it takes to get the job done, regardless of the consequences to your family and well-being. You also may find yourself resenting others because they don't work as hard as you do. If you have the need for duty or to do the right thing, make sure your company and your partner share your values, or you may find you are working at cross-purposes.

Like those with the need to accomplish, people who have a need for duty often sacrifice their health and well-being in an effort to fulfill their obligations and to satisfy others. It is important to fulfill this need in healthy ways and put in place good habits to maintain your health and well-being. After all, you can't fulfill your obligations if you aren't alive to do it.

Meeting the Need Through Others

- Ask five of your closest friends, family members, or colleagues to call you or write a card acknowledging who you are once a week for the next eight weeks. You need to learn that people value you for who you are, not just what you do, so that you are freed from having to do things for others out of duty or obligation.

- Set clear time limits and boundaries with your boss. If your boss proposes a Sunday morning meeting to prepare for a big presentation, let him or her know that you aren't available on weekends, but would be able to stay late or come in early to work on a special project. Make sure that your extended hours are the exception, not the rule. If a boss or colleague calls you at home, let him or her know that this is your private time and that you will be happy to discuss the issue in the morning.

- Ask your romantic partner to give you a massage or anything else that helps you feel relaxed.

- Ask your partner to go on walks or exercise with you. You may find that you do better if you are supporting your mate in one of his or her goals. For example, you may not care about your own health but will go on a healthy eating plan to support your partner. You might be motivated to run or walk to raise money for a charity.

Meeting the Need Yourself

- The best way to fulfill your need is to make sure that your sense of duty is aligned to your values and that your values are compatible with both your partner's and your company's. For example, if you have a strong sense of duty to your country, you might want to work for the government or the military. And obviously, don't marry a flag burner!

- Learn to say no and say it often. You have a natural inclination or sense of duty that others will take advantage of, so get comfortable saying no.

- Make your health a priority. You can't fulfill your duties or obligations if you aren't looking after yourself. Take a good multivitamin and reduce your caffeine intake if you feel stressed. Walk for at least twenty minutes every day. Meditate, write in a journal, or sit quietly and listen to music every day. It is important to take time for yourself.

Meeting Your Partner's Need

- Set firm and clear boundaries with your date or mate. For example, you might say, "Dinner is at 7:00 P.M. every night and I expect you to be here, no excuses." Or, "No one from work can call us in the evening or on weekends unless it is truly an emergency."

- Find a cause or organization that you both enjoy contributing to. Decide to commit to only one activity at a time so that you don't get overwhelmed. For example, you might both want to do something for the environment and might enjoy volunteering for a local cause or organization. This fulfills your partner's need for duty while at the same time enabling you to spend time together.

- Your partner may feel a stronger sense of duty to look after your health than his or her own. So ask your partner to support you in becoming fitter and healthier by going with you to the gym or walking together. My mother lost twenty-five pounds by supporting me to lose weight by doing the diet with me. Her duty to support her children is stronger than her duty to herself.

- Acknowledge your partner for who he or she is, not just for the things he or she does for you. For example, instead of saying, "Thanks for fixing the fence," try saying, "You are generous and loving." The more your partner knows he or she doesn't have to do something or prove himself or herself to merit your love and affection, the more you'll release the driving sense of duty.

Malcolm's Story. Malcolm has a tremendous sense of duty to his work. When he hired a coach he was working ninety hours a week, was hugely overweight, and had just come out of the hospital after a near and total collapse. His doctor told him that he would have to work less, lose weight, and take better care of his health or risk losing his life. It took this dramatic wake-up call before he would have even thought of hiring a coach. He admitted to looking down on those who hired coaches, but now found himself unable to make the changes he knew he had to make. Why was he so compelled to work every hour in the day? Why couldn't he take time for himself? As long as there was work to do, that took priority over everything, including his health and his family. His sense of duty and obligation drove him to the brink of death itself. Malcolm had given everything to his work. He never saw his family because he worked so late. His relationship with his two teenage boys was dysfunctional at best. When he spent time with his wife, he wasn't really present as he was thinking about his work, talking to his colleagues on his cell phone, or checking e-mails on weekends. He didn't really have a marriage—it was a sham. He was married completely to his work, driven by his overriding sense of duty.

His immediate goal was to cut his workweek down from ninety hours to fifty hours a week. To do this, Malcolm had to realign his sense of duty and make his self-care his first and primary concern. If he didn't take care of himself, he would be unable to fulfill any of his duties to work or family. He joined a gym and signed up with a personal trainer who also specialized in nutrition. He started making small changes to his diet and doing short twenty-minute walks on the treadmill at the gym. Gradually he added five minutes each week to his walks until he could walk for an hour. His next challenge was to unplug himself from his cell phone and computer on weekends. He found he didn't know what to do with himself when faced with all this time. He decided to spend some time with his sons and asked them what they liked to do. They went fishing together. Malcolm realized that he didn't know his own children. He didn't know what they liked to do, what their favorite color was, what their concerns and worries were. Free from his computer, he was finally available to be with his wife and children on weekends. He asked for his sons' support in his exercise campaign and they walked together through the woods. He started taking his wife out on proper dates again. He was fortunate that she was still there for him and all that his relationship needed was some time and attention.

Now Malcolm is working forty to fifty hours a week and takes his weekends completely off. He still feels a strong sense of duty, but he knows that his self-care must come first or he will be useless to those around him. He has discovered that he is more effective at work because he is rested and more efficient. Instead of disappointing his boss, he has been promoted, even though he is working almost half the time he did before. Malcolm has saved his life, his marriage, and his relationship with his children simply by understanding how his needs were driving him and then fulfilling them in healthy ways.

15. Right

Be Deferred to, Correct, Not Mistaken, Morally Right, Understood

If you have the need to be right, you might be perceived as a "know-it-all" or an intellectual. It bothers you tremendously and you'll avoid being wrong at all costs. You don't like being told you are wrong, especially in public and will often have the information or evidence to back up your point. In relationships, it can be very hard for you to lose an argument and you may even be a poor sport about it, sulking or becoming angry. You may expect your partner to back you up in front of others. At work, you might resist taking orders from someone you feel isn't right or is less intelligent than you are. You may be highly principled and believe that the world would be a better place if more people did the right thing or looked at the world the same way you do. You might have strong religious or spiritual convictions. You likely are unwilling to work for someone or an organization that you feel to be morally corrupt or unethical.

Meeting the Need Through Others

- Once a week for the next eight weeks ask a friend to call you and tell you one thing you are right about, for example, "Remember the time when x-y-z happened? Well, you were right about that." Or ask him or her to reinforce what you want to be right about.

- Ask your friends and family to acknowledge you when you are right. Tell them that it is OK to disagree with you, but that you'd like them to first say, "You are right. I can see from your point of view why that makes sense." Once your need to be right is satisfied, you'll find it is much easier to hear another point of view. Then they can go on to say, "Another point of view is . . ." and you are now ready to listen to them.

Meeting the Need Yourself

- Surround yourself with "yes men," encouraging people inspiring you to do your best. Why should you be around people who don't agree with you or support your plans or visions? Thomas Leonard, founder of Coach U and the "grandfather" of coaching, used to say that you should *only* surround yourself with these kinds of people. You can't afford to be around negative people who drain your energy. Does this mean you will never hear a contradictory point of view? No. It means that the people who disagree with you do so in a respectful way and honor your need to be right, even if you are wrong.

- Join an organization or club that supports your views.

Meeting Your Partner's Need

- Let your partner get the last word in at the end of an argument.

- If in a discussion or debate, always start by saying, "You are absolutely right." (Even if you disagree with him or her, you can honestly say this because, from your partner's perspective, he or she *is* right.) Once your mate's need to be right has been fulfilled, then he or she just might be able to hear a different point of view. For example, you might say, "You're right. (Long pause.) I can see from your point of view how you would come up with that. Another point of view is . . ." Avoid using the word *but* because it negates everything you just said prior to it. Don't say, "You are right, but . . ." Instead say, "You are right. And here is another point of view . . . " Using the word *and* is more inclusive of your partner's point of view and gives room for both perspectives.

- Agree to disagree on hot topics that invariably provoke an argument. It is OK to avoid topics on which you simply don't see eye to eye. If you are a Democrat and your partner is a Republican, have a policy that you won't discuss politics together. It isn't going to have a happy ending, so there is no point going there.

- Focus and redirect the conversation to areas and views you have in common, reinforcing and strengthening your bond as a couple.

Cecilia's Story. Cecilia had the need to be right. She couldn't stand to lose an argument and she always had to have the last word. She hated to be criticized, especially if the remark was in public. In relationships, she couldn't let a point drop. She would argue and argue until finally, out of exhaustion, her partner would relent and concede the point. To compound matters, Cecilia was extremely bright and articulate. More often than not, she *was* right. But the repercussions of this need were heavy. Her arrogance combined with her need to be right didn't win her any friends at the office. In spite of her brains and great talent, she was fired from her job for calling her boss an idiot.

The home front wasn't much better. Cecilia's partner had lost his voice. His opinion and his needs didn't matter. He eventually filed for divorce and left. Cecilia discovered it was a lonely world without the love and support of her partner. She started her own business so that she didn't have to take "stupid orders from idiots anymore." She started dating and this time, she was very up front about her need to be right and asked her date to "make her right" even if he disagreed. This worked well. Cecilia also joined Mensa where she can join in debates with others and typically wins the argument. This fulfills her need to the point where she feels sufficiently right that she doesn't have to win all the arguments at home. By meeting her needs sufficiently at work and in her social life, she is now a better partner and has attracted a man she really loves.

16. Security/Safety

Assurances, Commitments, Guarantees, Insurance, Protection, Reliability, Stability

People with the need for security typically require commitments. If you have the need for security, you probably won't feel comfortable being engaged without a definite wedding date or living together without a marriage certificate. To feel secure you need to know when things are happening and that they are being done properly. In relationships, you'll expect your partner to want the same level of commitment. You would probably feel insecure if your partner didn't want to commit to you and eventually marry you. You probably wouldn't want to live together without a commitment for an extended period of time. An open marriage would make you feel very uncomfortable. In relationships, you need exclusivity and probably wouldn't tolerate a partner who was sleeping around or dating others. At work, you'll want a steady paycheck or a contract that specifies your requirements and the commitments of your employer to you. You would probably feel uncomfortable working on a commission basis or as a freelancer. While someone with the need for freedom and independence might balk at signing a two- to five-year contract, you feel the longer it is, the better. You like working for a company with good benefits, especially medical. Financially, you'll prefer the security of a long-term mortgage as opposed to a short-term or variable interest mortgage. You prefer to buy products with solid or long-term guarantees or buying from companies with excellent service records in the event of any problem or defect. You need to know you can return a product for any reason. You may work hard to own your house outright, preferring to live in a smaller house you own than have a mortgage. You may need a solid financial reserve of a minimum of six months to two years of living expenses before you feel secure financially.

Meeting the Need Through Others

- Ask your closest family members and friends to tell you that they love you once a week for the next eight weeks so you can feel emotionally secure.

- Ask your boss for a written job description and get all conditions or requirements for bonuses and commissions in writing. Ask to sign a job contract.

- Get all agreements, especially with friends and family, in writing, even if this is as simple as "IOU $5" on a scrap of paper with a date and signature.

- Once you are ready to engage in a serious relationship, ask your partner what his or her commitment level is and make each other's expectations of the relationship clear from the beginning.

Meeting the Need Yourself

- Do not sleep with anyone unless he or she has agreed to be exclusive.

- Create financial security: meet with a financial planner to make sure you are on a solid financial path and have sufficient insurance to protect yourself; invest in stable, reputable financial institutions and secure funds; have a stable source of regular income and keep extra emergency cash on hand; regularly save at least 10 percent of your income; keep six months to two years of funds in a savings account.

- Make sure you are physically safe and secure: get a good security system installed in your home and make sure you have fire alarms and smoke detectors throughout the house; buy a car with good safety records and airbags and always wear your seatbelt; make sure you have a reliable emergency auto repair service; get everyone in your family to take a CPR course.

- Make sure your belongings are secure: put valuables and important documents in a safe-deposit box; use a credit card with the best buyer's protection insurance; buy quality products with good guarantees; install an automatic backup system for your computer.

- Work for a reputable company with excellent benefits, and if you are self-employed, get as much disability insurance as you can.

- Keep a supply of extra batteries for your phone, computer, or other gadgets on hand.

Meeting Your Partner's Need

- Book your dates in advance, at least by Wednesday if not sooner for a weekend date. Do not wait until the last minute to make plans. It will make him or her feel insecure. Tell your date where you'll be going and what you'll be doing, and if it is a surprise, make sure you give enough details so that he or she feels comfortable and knows what to wear.

- Don't be offended by your partner's request for a prenuptial agreement. It may be what he or she needs to feel secure in the relationship.

- Ask your date or mate what he or she needs to feel secure. Would he or she like you to call once a day at lunchtime or in the evening? Perhaps your partner prefers an old-fashioned love letter expressing your sentiments.

Wendy's Story. Wendy hired me because she wanted to quit her job and start her own business but she was afraid to do so. At thirty-three years of age, she also wanted to find a great man to marry and raise a family with. She was dating a very generous, loving man in his early fifties, but he already had grown children of his own and wasn't interested in having another family. He did love her very much and had repeatedly asked her to marry him. She kept putting him off because she really wanted to have children, but she couldn't seem to break up with him either. Wendy was stuck both personally and professionally and it was her need for security that kept her stuck. She was afraid to quit her job because she didn't know if she'd have enough money, and she was afraid to leave the security of this cozy relationship. What if there was no one better out there?

Since the only way to make a need go away is to fulfill it, we started working on ways to make her feel more secure. Wendy was already a good saver and started saving even more, cutting back on unnecessary expenses so that she would have a solid reserve to fund her new business. She decided to keep her day job and work on her business in the evenings and weekends. This was a smart move as it took much longer to develop a client base than she anticipated. Then, the hard part: she had to break up with this loving and gentle man. As much as she loved him, they didn't share the same life goals. She broke up with him very gracefully, explaining that she loved him but couldn't marry him because she wanted a man who was ready to have a family.

Next we looked again at her finances, and she realized she had enough money invested that she could safely quit her job and start her own business, with five years' worth of living expenses. Still she didn't feel comfortable tapping into her savings, so she took on part-time work while building her business. Once she felt secure financially, she attracted a man just two years older who wanted a family as well. The only problem was that he didn't have the financial security she had hoped for. They dated a few years while she was growing her business and he paid off his debts. She realized she loved him regardless of how much money he had and that she was willing to be the big bread winner in the family. Wendy realizes that it is up to her to create her own security in the family, and her husband doesn't mind that she makes more money than he does. They recently married and are now living very happily together. Now that they've made it through the first year, they are thinking about starting their family.

17. Supported

Be Attended to, Cared for, Embraced, Given Gifts,
Helped, Looked After, Nurtured, Provided for,
Saved, Taken Care of, Treasured, Welcomed

If you need to be supported or cared for, you may attract a mate or partner who has the complementary need to be needed or to be of service. This actually can make a nice fit, provided that you appreciate your partner's efforts, don't overburden him or her, and share a value or two in common as well. You like to be looked after, catered to, attended, and, if you are a woman, you probably like having the car door opened for you when appropriate. If you are a man, you would probably prefer a more traditional wife who looks after you, cooks for you, brings you your coffee and paper in the morning, and otherwise attends to your well-being and comfort. If you are a woman, you might be drawn to a man who can provide for you financially as well as emotionally—someone who looks after you with tenderness and affection and brings you flowers and other gifts—a true gentleman who is courteous and thoughtful. At work, you may find you do your best when you have an excellent assistant to support you and handle administrative details and tasks. A supportive manager or supervisor will help to make you feel cared for and taken care of at work.

Meeting the Need Through Others

- Ask five of your closest friends and family members to do one thing a week for the next eight weeks to demonstrate to you that they care for you. You could ask them to send or bring a small gift or flowers, to cook you a dinner, or take you out for a surprise event.

- Ask your assistant to bring you coffee or tea in the morning.

- If meeting a friend or colleague for lunch, offer to treat this time and suggest that they can treat the next time. (It feels much nicer and more civilized than splitting the tab.)

- Ask your romantic partner for a regular foot or back massage. Set it up so that he or she does this weekly without asking.

- If your date insists on paying for meals out, thank him or her graciously and let him or her know you feel very cared for. You can respond by cooking dinner at home or getting tickets to the theater or some other treat.

- Ask the men in your life to open doors for you and pull out your chair, and let them know that you prefer to be treated like a lady.

- Ask your date to make the reservations and handle the logistics on your dates, always letting him or her know that it makes you feel cared for.

- Hire a life coach who will support you in reaching your goals and objectives.

Meeting the Need Yourself

- Choose a naturally thoughtful, giving, and generous partner who cares for you and all those he or she loves.

- Surround yourself with gentle, loving, and supportive people.

- Ask for what you need from people and thank them graciously.

- Hire help: a housekeeper, a personal trainer to workout with, a handyman to come once a month to fix things around the house and yard, or a kid from the neighborhood to mow your lawn.

- Do one thing a day to pamper yourself (hot bubble bath, time to write in your journal or meditate, a walk in the park, etc.).

- Discard, repair, or replace anything and everything that is worn, stained, chipped, or broken.

- Go to a spa or sign up for a spa-like gym where you can take a regular sauna or steam. Get a weekly manicure or pedicure or get a regular massage.

- Book an all-inclusive holiday at a place like Club Med where they have mastered the art of taking care of you and you just show up, relax, and enjoy.

Meeting Your Partner's Need

- Ask your date or mate how he or she likes to be treated. For example, does she like having doors opened or does she prefer to do it herself?

- Treat your romantic partner to dinners and meals out or send flowers, gifts, chocolates, and so forth.

- Leave little sticky notes around the house or tucked into a briefcase with a sentiment of appreciation or loving thought.

- Bring your mate coffee or tea in bed, just the way he or she likes it.

- Let your partner sleep in while you get the kids ready for school.

- Have a refreshing drink or cocktail ready when your partner returns from work.

- Make sure the house is tidy and fresh.

- Greet your mate with a kiss and a hug.

- Run the bath for him or her and lay out a robe and towel.

Leslie's Story. Leslie had the need to be taken care of and looked after, yet she continually found that she was in relationships with men who wanted and expected her to do the looking after, as, culturally, many men expect the women in their lives to do the nurturing. Leslie wrote a very specific list of the things she wanted in a man and the ways she wanted to be taken care of, including a man who would be happy to make her a cup of tea and bring it to her in bed and take time off from work if she was sick to look after her. She started looking for a real gentleman, the sort who would open doors and who was very thoughtful and considerate. And she found him! He loves looking after her and does this naturally because it gives him joy and pleasure. If this is one of your needs, it makes sense to find someone who loves to nurture and care for people.

18. Touched

Caressed, Connected, Cuddled, Held, Hugged, Kissed, Massaged, Stroked

While the need for human contact is universal, some people need a lot more touching, holding, cuddling, and caressing than others. If you have the need to touch you are probably seen as a warm, affectionate, or even cuddly person. In relationships, you'll never feel completely satisfied or connected to your partner if you don't get sufficient cuddling, holding, or touching. You are often the one reaching out to touch others, the one who greets everyone with a big hug and a kiss. There are also cultural differences to be aware of. Italians touch, hug, and kiss much more than Germans, for example. If you come from a culture or family where a lot of touching or hugging is normal, you might feel the lack of touching if your partner comes from a less cuddly culture. You may need to gradually introduce your partner to your customs and expectations. Some people strongly dislike being touched except by their romantic partner or spouse, so this is not something you should do to people you don't know well. Avoid asking people at work to meet this need unless it is completely appropriate.

Meeting the Need Through Others

- Ask family members and close friends to give you a big hug or a gentle hold whenever they come to visit or see you.

- Ask your partner to hold or cuddle with you for a set amount of time each night. As a couple, you can set a specific amount of time that you both agree on.

- Ask for lots of cuddling and caressing before and after sex.

- Generally it is best to avoid asking work colleagues to do this as it can be seen as too personal and intimate and may be misconstrued or inappropriate. In some cases, it might even be considered sexual harassment. However, if you are in a touchy-feely environment, it might be perfectly appropriate. Use your good judgment and common sense and if you have any doubts at all, always ask permission first.

Meeting the Need Yourself

- Book a weekly massage with a great therapist who really makes you feel terrific. Experiment with different types of massage (Reiki, sports, Swedish, reflexology, etc.) until you find the right one. Don't settle for anything less than marvelous, as different strokes work for different folks. This is critical if you are single and not in a romantic relationship as you probably aren't getting this need sufficiently met.

- Surround yourself with touchy-feely, warm, and affectionate people. Consider finding and joining a community where the people are naturally affectionate and want touching and holding, such as a home for the elderly, a children's hospital, a church group, or an animal rescue shelter.

- Choose a partner who is a cuddly sort of person and naturally fulfills your need.

- Never have sex with someone just to get this need fulfilled.

- Give your date or mate a big hug and a kiss every day before and after work.

- Take a massage or reflexology class together so that you fulfill this need on a regular basis and learn the skills to relax each other with touch.

- Show your date or mate exactly how to do it so that it fulfills your need. Some people like gentle holds while others prefer big bear hugs and squeezes. Some people like their scalp and back raked with fingernails and others like a gentle caress. Make sure you are specific and show your partner exactly how you like it as there is no way he or she will know unless you demonstrate.

Meeting Your Partner's Need

- Ask your date or mate how he or she would like to be touched. Does he or she want a big bear hug or a tender hold? Does your partner like a back scratch with fingernails or an oily massage?

- Make sure you cuddle or hold your partner before and after sex.

- Surprise your partner with a gift certificate for a massage as often as you can afford to.

- Take a massage class and learn how the pros do it and use your mate to practice your newfound skills.

- Whenever you have the chance, give a minimassage for a minute or two. If your partner is seated at a computer, give him or her a gentle shoulder rub.

Jennifer's Story. Jennifer is a forty-something divorced mother of a teenage boy. She lives in a small town in the mountains and works from home. Now that her son has gone away to college, she is all alone in the house and feeling very lonely. She signed up for coaching in the hopes of getting out of her rut and finding a great relationship. She loves her work and her home but feels she is too isolated and doesn't know where she can meet people in such a small town. We discussed her emotional needs and she realized she has the need to be touched. She used to get big hugs from her son on a daily basis, but now that he is away, she hasn't had a hug, let alone a kiss or a cuddle, in ages.

I encouraged Jennifer to satisfy her need to be touched immediately by getting a weekly massage. She found a fellow who was training at a local massage school and needed someone to practice on. Jennifer happily volunteered to be his guinea pig. I also asked her to find a friend who was willing to hold her—a girlfriend could do this. Jennifer told her friend that she was embarrassed to ask, but that living alone, she had no hugs. Would she be willing to hold her tenderly a few minutes? Her friend was honored to be asked and now, whenever she meets Jennifer, she gives her a big, long hug. We quickly determined that Jennifer would need to get exposure to eligible men and it wasn't going to happen in her local community as most of the men were either married already, retired, or otherwise not eligible. She had to find a few ways to meet eligible men and started Internet dating. After weeding out a number of candidates, she has found a few that look like good potential mates and is now starting to date them.

19. Useful/Needed

Care for or Look After Others, Give, Be Helpful, Indispensable, Serve

If you have the need to be needed, you are likely to be a selfless, generous, and caring person. You get genuine pleasure out of helping or taking care of others. You often go out of your way to help a friend or neighbor in need. You are very kind, thoughtful, and giving. You seek ways to help people and go to great lengths to help when asked a favor. In relationships, you are great at supporting your partner in his or her goals and objectives and will give selflessly of your time and energy. You would make a wonderful parent as you enjoy caring for your children's needs. In relationships, this need can complement the need to be loved, cherished, or cared for very nicely. At work, you may find yourself happiest in one of the caring professions such as being a doctor, nurse, caretaker, firefighter, homemaker, teacher, counselor, social worker, executive assistant, or caterer. If you get pleasure from taking care of others, then find people who want to be taken care of. However, if you suspect your relationship is becoming codependent or unhealthy in any way, then immediately seek the help of a good therapist or counselor.

Meeting the Need Through Others

- Let family, friends, and colleagues know how you are willing to help them and ask for what you need in return. For example, "I'm happy to babysit the grandchildren every week, but I would appreciate it if you would pick me up and take me home afterward or if you could provide dinner for me." People with the need to serve are often taken for granted by friends and family. It is important that you make sure you aren't making any painful sacrifices in order to help. Set firm and clear boundaries with your time and resources.

- Tell your friends, family, and colleagues how you would like them to acknowledge your contributions and service. Be specific. You might want them to say something like, "Thanks for your help. I couldn't do it without your support!"

- Offer to help or volunteer at a favorite local charity, hospital, or church group.

- Make a double batch of whatever you are cooking and bring a portion to someone who has suffered a death or is sick and needs looking after.

Meeting the Need Yourself

- Choose a partner who appreciates you and never takes you or the support you give for granted.

- Learn to say no if asked to do something you do not wish to do.

- Tell people how they can thank you or appreciate you for your help, and learn to accept people's thanks graciously.

- Tell your boss and colleagues how to appreciate you.

- Set boundaries with your time and let people know when it is OK to call or visit.

- If you aren't already in a helping or service profession, you might find that this need disappears when you do something that you really feel is making a difference. It is worth getting the training to switch careers.

■ If you like your work but it doesn't fulfill this need, volunteer for a charity or organization that you care about. Volunteer at the hospital, a retirement home, or an animal shelter.

■ Book a charity holiday or vacation where you donate your time, money, or expertise to a charity for a week or two in a developing country.

Meeting Your Partner's Need

■ Thank your partner for all of his or her help and support. Show your appreciation by giving him or her a handwritten note of thanks, a big hug, or whatever feels appropriate. Do this often. The more gratitude you express, the more likely your partner will be to offer more help in the future.

■ Be aware that your date or mate might offer to help when he or she really can't afford the time or money. People with the need to be needed are selfless and will put themselves out to help. Make sure your partner is taking care of himself or herself and not just looking after you. For example, you might say, "Yes, I'd love it if you helped me with this, but only after you've had a nap."

■ Tell your partner up front when it is OK to say no to something you request. If you want your partner to pick up the dry cleaning you might say, "If you have the time, please pick up the dry cleaning on the way home. If not, I can get it tomorrow."

Ralph's Story. Ralph couldn't say no if someone asked him for help. He was so busy taking care of others that he neglected his own health and well-being. He joked that a forty-hour workweek was a holiday for him. And it wasn't just the fact that he owned three businesses. He worked long hours because if an acquaintance called and asked for his help or advice, he freely helped even if that meant putting his own work aside to do later in the evening. He had no boundaries around his time because he genuinely loved helping others, but after surviving two heart attacks, he had to stop. His doctor insisted that he cut his workweek down to thirty-five hours a week. He knew he couldn't say no; he knew he had to or he wouldn't live to see his ten-year-old son grow up. That is when Ralph finally decided to hire me.

We started with some basic boundaries. He had to leave the office at 5:00 P.M. no matter what. If friends or colleagues called for help, he would tell them he could give them five minutes of time. I asked him to set a real timer so that he wouldn't lose track of time. When it rang, he would have to end the conversation by gently and firmly saying, "It was great talking to you, Joe. I've got to get back to work now." Ralph found that he could offer a lot of help in a short period of time by setting a time limit. This one tactic saved him ten to twenty hours a week.

He also began to spend time training his staff to do the job properly. This way he felt in control, knowing they would do a better job than he would. He discovered that his staff was actually perfectly capable of doing the job. This freed up another twenty hours a week. He was down to forty hours and getting more done with less effort. His doctor was pleased and his wife and son were thrilled that they had more time with him as well. Ralph found that by being selfish about getting his own needs met, those around him were better taken care of as well. His staff was happier and more motivated now that they were given some real work to do, and his family was happier to have him at home for dinner. When those around him were happier, he felt happier. It was a win-win for all.

20. Win

Be First, Be the Best, Conquer, Defeat, Master, Overcome, Persuade, Succeed, Take the Prize, Triumph, Vanquish, Victory

If to win is your need, you'll work and play hard to be the winner and you might not be a very good loser. You have a natural desire to be the best in every situation both personally and professionally. In relationships, you'll probably be happiest if you are the better "catch." It can work for you to marry a supportive person who appreciates that you are just a bit ahead—brighter, smarter, wealthier—and lets you take the lead. In other words, it is understood that your career comes first. You'll come to conflict if you both need to win in a relationship. Your competitive streak drives you to push yourself harder than the next person. You'll do whatever it takes to come out on top.

Meeting the Need Through Others

- Master a game and then have a weekly party where you can play full out. A great poker player hosted weekly poker parties with his friends. More often than not, he was the winner, ending the evening with real cash and his need to win completely fulfilled. A client used to play Bunko with her women friends and had a great time while also fulfilling her need to win. Get this need fulfilled in ways that are fun for you.

- Join a tennis, golf, racquetball, or sports club where you can regularly win games or tournaments.

- There is nothing wrong with picking less talented opponents so you can ensure that you'll win. After all, the point is to get your need met! If you think this is unfair, remember you are doing a service to the other players by giving them a challenge.

- If you like to win mental challenges, try sudoku or other brain teasers.

Meeting the Need Yourself

- Avoid marrying your equal or better. Or at least, make sure you feel superior to your mate and your mate likes it this way. This may sound terrible, but in truth, women have been told to "marry up" for years. I once read a book by an Australian woman who said that if you marry someone who is better educated, has a better job, and is smarter and wealthier, then you are putting yourself in an inferior position from the start. When choices are made, his career will be more important, his choices will be better, and so forth. This was an eye-opener for me because I wanted an equal partnership. I didn't want to be the subordinate one. If you want an equal partnership, then marry someone who is an equal, not your superior. And, if you have the need to win, you may find that you are happier being the more accomplished one. Marrying "up" may not be a good idea if you are a woman with the need to win or be the best. Or you could solve the problem by marrying someone who is "the best" at the things you don't mind. Perhaps your husband has a better education, but you are the better musician. Or marry someone who is accomplished without a competitive spirit.

- Set realistic and achievable goals that require you to stretch and challenge yourself but also enable you to win.

- Keep a running log of all your wins (a modern-day version of the notch on the belt).

- Convert rejections into wins. For example, one sales executive hated getting rejected when making calls. I suggested he figure out how many "no's" he would have to get before he would get one "yes." In order to sell one widget, he estimated that he would have to call an average of fifty companies. He needed to collect forty-nine "no's" before he'd get one sale. Instead of counting the "yes's", he started counting the "no's" as a win. "Yeah! I just got a 'no'—only forty-eight left to go!" A bit of a mind game, but sales can really be demoralizing, so this works to keep the focus positive.

- Likewise, instead of getting completely disheartened by a series of rejection letters during his job hunt, a fellow student made it a game and started posting them on the dormitory walls for everyone to see (a red badge of courage). He must have posted about thirty-five letters before he landed a job. His victory was even sweeter because this quest engaged the rest of us.

Meeting Your Partner's Need

- If your partner is getting discouraged, see if you can't find the wins within the quest and make it a game.

- Work with your partner to set realistic and achievable goals. For example, decide that you'll save $250 a month as a couple. Then if you save $300, you've beat the goal and won.

- The gold star method is great. Give your partner a gold star on the calendar for every day he or she wins. Ask your mate to decide what the objective is (for example, not smoking, walking the dog, eating all her vegetables). This may sound silly, but it *does* work for adults, not just kids. My sister-in-law has a star chart on the wall with a large section for her two daughters and a smaller section for her husband—he is working on putting his dirty laundry in the basket instead of on the floor. And, it works. He gets a treat each week for perfect results just like the girls. His first reward was "peace and quiet," so he took the morning off to read the paper at the coffee shop. This handily fulfilled his need for peace and his wife's need for order.

Anna's Story. Anna, a thirty-two-year-old accountant, had a big need to win. She had a strong competitive streak both personally and professionally. She worked long and hard to achieve professional success, but she had greater difficulty in relationships. Anna couldn't help but find herself trying to win men over. She was trying too hard and, as a result, ended up pushing the men she was most interested in away. Once in a relationship, she had to be the best. When she realized her need to win was driving her to compete with her dates, she laughed. It was time to find some healthier ways to fulfill her need. She decided to set up a weekly bridge game with a group of girlfriends as a release for her competitive streak. This worked really well as she was a good player and usually won. Her friends enjoyed the fun and company and didn't mind that she usually won.

With her needs fulfilled, she no longer had to compete with her dates and soon attracted an incredibly handsome man, a professional bodybuilder and personal trainer who absolutely adored her. And as they weren't in the same field, she didn't feel the need to compete with him. He was successful in his own right. When she worked too hard and long, he playfully scooped her up and escorted her to the bedroom for a "break." They are now happily married and he still scoops her up and whisks her upstairs, much to her dismay and ultimate delight.

21. Work

Be Busy, Be Industrious, Do Tasks, Exercise, Have a Career or Vocation, Labor, Make It Happen, Perform, Produce, Take Action

If you can't stand sitting around relaxing and really prefer to be busy doing something, you probably have a need to work or be busy. If you book a vacation, it won't be to lie around on a beach drinking margaritas. You would much rather be up and about seeing the sights or taking a scuba-diving lesson. If you are on vacation at a family member's house, you might find you get bored, irritable, and restless if you don't have a project to work on. You might be happier if you could paint the garden fence or make a lasagna. You are great to have around because you get things done. But, your drive to keep busy might make others uncomfortable if they feel they have to keep pace with you when they want to relax or do nothing. The important thing to understand is that, for you, work is relaxing. In relationships, you'll do well to allow your mate to have some time off to do nothing. Let your partner know you don't expect him or her to keep pace with you. You'll want to find a career that is a match for your values and then you'll be very happy as both your need to work and your values will be fulfilled. You may be perceived as a workaholic. Make sure you put in place systems to take care of your health and well-being and devote time to your relationships as well.

Meeting the Need Through Others

- When you are visiting parents or friends' houses, tell them you prefer staying busy and ask if they have any projects you could work on. Give them some suggestions as to what you could do. (My sister and brother-in-law redecorated my mother's bathroom when they were visiting over Christmas.)

Meeting the Need Yourself

- Bring a portable project with you when traveling, such as knitting, writing, or sketching.

- Choose work that is fulfilling and in alignment with at least one of your top values.

- Set clear boundaries around your work to avoid letting work interfere with family time.

- Take excellent care of your health and well-being.

- Have special projects, tasks, and hobbies that fulfill your need at home as well as at work.

Meeting Your Partner's Need

- Give your romantic partner a list of things he or she can work on around the house.

- Find a shared value-based goal and create a project to work on together.

- Don't take your partner's need to work personally, but do set clear boundaries around working hours. For example, "Dinner will be on the table at 7:00 P.M. every night, and I expect you to be home in time."

- Encourage and support your partner in his or her vocation or career.

- Understand that your date or mate probably can't sit still for long. It isn't personal; he or she relaxes by doing something.

- Book a vacation that offers a variety of activities.

Michael's Story. Michael has the need to work, to be busy and industrious. On top of that, he is a perfectionist. When he worked in construction, he relentlessly put in eighty to ninety hours a week. He was promoted to site manager. When he takes a vacation, he likes to have a project to do such as learn how to scuba dive, climb mountains, or go skiing. He can't stand the thought of lying on a beach doing nothing for a week. After about fifteen minutes he is up and about, looking for something to do. Michael's need helped drive him to be successful in work, but it made relationships difficult. He didn't have time to even find a woman, much less date her. When I pointed out that if he didn't have a free half hour for a coaching call three times a month, then he certainly didn't have the time for a relationship. He had to stop filling up his calendar with work and start making some space for love. I urged him to set aside three evenings a week without plans. He needed to have a little space in order to even notice the women around him. Sure enough, within a month, he had attracted a great lady, they started dating, and they are now married.

However, Michael hadn't completely solved the problem. Once he was married, he got right back to work and didn't take time off to play with her. She felt neglected and unloved because he worked so much. Even when he came home from work, he then started a project on the house that took his evenings and weekends. His need to work seemed insatiable. Michael realized that this wasn't fair to his partner and that he needed to spend time with her to maintain a good relationship. It isn't something you can just tick off a list. To solve the problem, they put in place a weekly date night, and it is Michael's job to pick the restaurant or plan the activity, which he enjoys because he likes being busy. I suggested that they both enroll in a fun class or activity that they can enjoy taking together, so they signed up for a swing dancing class. This has worked really well, fulfilling Michael's need to be busy and his wife's need to have fun.

So, there you have it—the top twenty-one needs. Feel free to use your own ideas, and remember that there are countless ways to get your needs fulfilled. The ones I've cited are just to get you thinking about how your own needs might be affecting your life and relationships. As you get your needs fulfilled you'll naturally attract the right relationships and opportunities to you. I recommend that you keep your top four needs posted and visible until you get completely comfortable asking your mate, friends, and family to fulfill them on a regular basis. I can predict right now that you'll probably be keen to meet the needs yourself but be very reluctant to ask someone else to meet them. You can only go so far with this program if you don't break through the fear, reluctance, squeamishness, or whatever you experience when you consider asking someone else to fulfill your needs. Asking very specifically for what you need is the secret to success, not just in dating and finding the right relationship but also in keeping your relationship going strong over the years.

7

· · · · · · · ·

Identify Your Core Values

NOW THAT YOU have identified your personal and emotional needs and have gotten them fulfilled to the point of disappearing altogether, it is time to take a look at your values—the things that are most important to you and that you love to do. Talk to any relationship expert or anyone married for years and they will tell you that the secret to success, the "glue" that keeps them together over the years and creates lasting love, is shared values. If you want a love that will work for the long run, then you'll definitely want to make sure you share at least one top value. The more values that you share with your mate, the more likely you are to have a long-lasting, fulfilling life together. While some of my clients have resisted doing the emotional needs work, they all enjoy the values work, because we love our values. Values give our life meaning, joy, and happiness. Our values and peak experiences are the source of profound fulfillment, passion, bliss, and even euphoria. If you aren't happy in your current relationship and your needs are fulfilled, then it may be that you need to start living your values. Get the passion back into your life!

And, if you want to attract the right man or woman to you, live your values. We are irresistible when we are doing what we love to do. I was leading a three-day coaching skills seminar in

London when I met my husband-to-be. I didn't know it then, of course, but afterward I realized that my mother had always said I'd find the right man when I was out there "doing my thing" leading and inspiring others.

One client, a very bodacious forty-year-old lawyer in New York, was struggling to find a man in the city. I kept urging her to travel to the places she always wanted to go. She wanted to travel with a man or even a girlfriend but eventually decided to take a two-week trip to Italy on her own. She came back with her husband in tow! Do what you love and your mate will be drawn to you as irresistibly as a moth is drawn to the light.

What Are Your True Passions?

· · · · · · · ·

What makes you feel turned on and excited about life? What are your passions? What has you bouncing out of bed in the morning, eager to start the day? These are our core values, and when we are living them regularly, we feel excited about life and radiate energy and enthusiasm. You are most likely to attract the ideal partner when you are fully living and expressing your core values. If you keep hitting the snooze button every morning or need multiple cups of coffee to motivate yourself to start the day, you aren't doing what you love to do. When we love our work and our life, we are naturally motivated to do it. You won't need artificial stimuli to get out of bed and get started. If you do not have a great life now and are waiting for the right partner, think again. You are responsible for your own happiness. If you rely on someone else to make you happy, what will happen when that person tires of doing so? The best way to attract a great relationship is to not need one (hence the needs work) and to be living a glorious life without the person (the values work). If you aren't totally thrilled with your life, then there is work to do!

The Peak Experiences Method

· · · · · · · · ·

One of the easiest ways to figure out what your passions and values are is to think about the best times of your life. Imagine for a moment that you are about to be hit by a bus and your whole life flashes before your eyes. You take out a yellow highlighter and color in the best times in your life. What would those be? Write down whatever comes to mind, whether that is something that occurred years ago or just recently. Think back through your entire life, including your childhood. Here is a sample list to get you thinking:

Highlights and Peak Experiences

1. Hiking in Malaysia
2. Riding a fast horse on the beach in Mexico
3. Giving the high school graduation speech
4. Living abroad for one year in Spain
5. Playing in the mud when I was a little kid
6. Taking a road trip around the United States
7. Going to Greece with my sister
8. Seeing the Grand Canyon
9. Dancing the waltz perfectly to a live band
10. Taking a weeklong yoga retreat
11. Camping in the Arizona mountains

12. Volunteering for the Fresh Air Fund

13. Tutoring El Salvadoran refugees in English

14. Running the New York marathon

15. Taking an enlightening personal development course

16. Taking a creative drawing or painting class

17. Enjoying an excellent meal out with friends

18. Christmas at Grandma's house

The Highlights and Peak Experiences of My Life
(write as many as you can possibly think of)

1. _____

2. _____

3. _____

4. _____

5. _____

6. _____

7. _____

8. _____

9. _____

10. _____

11. _____

12. _____

13. _____

14. _____

15. _____

16. _____

17. _____

18. _____

Now that you've jotted down a few highlights, set this list aside for a few minutes and we'll come back to it.

The Envy Method

· · · · · · · ·

Envy is one of the seven deadly sins, but I actually find it a very useful method for discovering your deeper desires, dreams, and values. Envy very precisely reveals what you secretly wish you could have or be yourself. What you envy in others is what you want for yourself. Who do you envy? What do you envy them for? Is it something they have, a quality or characteristic they possess, or something they have achieved? In what ways do you want to be like them, have what they have, or do what they are doing? This is an excellent indication of your own passions and values. If you are hankering after something somebody else has, then this is what you want for yourself. Make a list of all the people you envy and what specifically you want that they have. Also consider those you admire and what it is you admire about them. We often admire others for what we want to be, do, or have as well. However, we may admire qualities or abilities in another that we don't want for ourselves. For example, you might admire Tiger Woods's ability with the golf club but may have no interest in becoming a golfer yourself. In those instances, envy is sometimes a better indicator of what you really want. Following is a sample Envy list:

People I Envy/Admire	What I Want That They Have
1. Oprah Winfrey	Phenomenal wealth and influence
2. Bill Clinton	Charisma
3. Dalai Lama	Peace/awareness/spirituality
4. Colleague	Bestselling author/fame
5. My mother	Generosity
6. My sister	Kindness
7. My best friend	Laughter

Now make your own list.

People I Envy/Admire	What I Want That They Have
1. _____	
2. _____	
3. _____	
4. _____	
5. _____	
6. _____	
7. _____	
8. _____	
9. _____	
10. _____	

The Qualities and Characteristics List

· · · · · · · ·

The following is a fairly extensive list of qualities and characteristics that people often value. Read through the list and circle any words that jump off the page at you, excite you, or that you envy or admire in another and wish you could have as well. You may already have this quality and would like to expand it or orient your life around it. You can pull out the qualities you want from your Envy list above to get started. Feel free to add your own if it isn't listed here.

Abundance	Acceptance	Accountability
Accomplished	Adaptable	Adventurous
Affectionate	Alert	Appreciative
Articulate	Artistic	Audacious
Authentic	Aware	Beautiful
Blissful	Bold	Brave
Capable	Caring	Charitable
Cheerful	Cleanliness	Comfort
Concern	Confidence	Consideration
Cooperative	Compassionate	Connected
Constructive	Content	Contributing
Courageous	Courteous	Creative
Curious	Daring	Dedicated
Dependable	Desirous	Determined
Devoted	Discerning	Dramatic
Eagerness	Elegance	Encouraging
Endurance	Enlightened	Entertaining
Ethical	Enthusiastic	Energetic
Experimental	Expert	Exploring
Fairness	Faithful	Famous
Family-oriented	Forgiving	Frankness
Friendly	Freedom	Frugality

Fun	Funny	Generous
Gentle	Genuine	Glamorous
Glowing	Graceful	Gratitude
Happiness	Harmony	Health
Helpfulness	Honesty	Hope
Holiness	Holistic	Hospitality
Humor	Impartiality	Imaginative
Influential	Innocence	Inquisitive
Inspiring	Integrity	Intelligence
Inventive	Involvement	Inquisitive
Joyful	Just	Judicious
Kindness	Knowledgeable	Knowing
Laughter	Lighthearted	Listening
Loving	Loyal	Magnanimous
Mastery	Masterful	Merciful
Nurturing	Open-minded	Optimism
Order	Originality	Passionate
Patient	Peaceful	Perceptive
Perfection	Perseverance	Persuasive
Playful	Poise	Presence
Prosperity	Punctuality	Purpose
Radiance	Refined	Relaxation
Reliable	Religious	Responsible
Resourceful	Reverent	Robust
Romantic	Rugged	Satisfied
Secure	Self-respect	Self-control
Self-disclosing	Self-esteem	Sensitive
Sensuality	Serenity	Sexy
Sincerity	Sobriety	Spirited
Spiritual	Spontaneous	Sporty
Strong	Stylish	Successful
Supportive	Surrendering	Sympathetic
Tactful	Tasteful	Tenderness
Thoughtful	Tolerant	Trusting

Trustworthy	Truthful	Understanding
Vital	Visionary	Vulnerable
Wealthy	Wholeness	Wisdom
Worthiness	Zeal	

Narrow down this list to the top ten qualities you would most like to embody, express, and live by. (This exercise is important for attracting and selecting the right relationship, so write this down now.)

Top Ten Qualities and Characteristics of Being

1. _____

2. _____

3. _____

4. _____

5. _____

6. _____

7. _____

8. _____

9. _____

10. _____

The Values and Passions List

· · · · · · · ·

Another way to discover your values and passions is by creating a list of what you most want to do. Review the list of values below and circle the words that leap out at you as things you'd love your life to be about. If you'd bounce out of bed in the morning to do it, that is a good indication it is a core value. You can circle the heading or subheadings, it doesn't matter; just select as many values as appeal to you. In other words, if you could wake up and do what you most desired, what would it be? Imagine that money is no object. This is *not* the time to be practical or realistic. Just pick what makes your heart sing.

The following list of passions and values are mostly verbs or are action-oriented words. These are the things we most want to *do* in life. You might notice that there is some overlap with the list of needs. The difference between a need and a value is that you must fulfill your needs or there will be a negative consequence. For example, if you don't win, you might get crabby or irritable. However, if to win is one of your values, that means that you'd love your life to be about winning or would like to win on a regular basis. If you don't win, it isn't the end of the world, but you prefer to. In other words, our needs are a requirement for us to be our best whereas our values are about ultimate fulfillment in life—that is where we feel we are fulfilling our destiny, living our purpose, excited about life, and naturally energized. When we are expressing our values, we are naturally turned on about our life and we eagerly embrace any work there is to do. While fulfilling our needs creates a sense of satisfaction and contentment, fulfilling our values leads to euphoria, bliss, happiness, and joy—not something you'd want to miss out on!

- ■ **Adventure.** Traveling to foreign countries, exploring the unknown, camping, meeting new people, taking big risks, starting your own business, betting or gambling, playing poker or card games, doing physically dangerous or challenging activities such as bungee jumping, sky diving, mountain climbing, rapelling, ice camping, scuba diving

Chance	Challenge	Danger
Dare	Gamble	Endeavor
Enterprise	Experiment	Exhilaration
Explore	Hazard	Journey
Pioneer	Quest	Risk
Roam	Speculate	Travel
The Unknown	Thrill	Venture
Wager	Wander	

- **Seeking Beauty.** Spending time in nature, seeing art exhibits, galleries, and museums, decorating your home, antique hunting, designing a beautiful wardrobe, looking as attractive as possible, listening to music, going to concerts, living in a beautiful location or area, eating at the best restaurants, surrounding yourself with luxury, renovating a home, making something beautiful, being a stylist, hairdresser, artist, sculptor, painter, musician

Artistic	Attractive	Beautify
Civilize	Cultivate	Culture
Decorate	Enhance	Elegance
Elaborate	Embellish	Freshen
Gloriousness	Improve	Loveliness
Magnificence	Nature	Perfect
Polish	Radiance	Refine
Reform	Renovate	Taste
Transform		

- **Catalyze.** Coaching, mentoring, speaking, writing, persuading, leading, lobbying, managing a team, encouraging others to move forward in any way, tutoring, volunteering

Alter	Animate	Arouse	Coach
Encourage	Energize	Excite	Exhilarate
Exhort	Galvanize	Impact	Impassion
Impel	Incite	Influence	Instigate

Lobby	Motivate	Move	Persuade
Prompt	Spark	Spur	Touch
Transform	Turn on	Urge	Stimulate

- **Contribute.** Volunteering for a charity, tutoring children or adults, visiting or caring for disabled, sick, or elderly, helping others, being a minister or volunteer in a church or other community service, coaching, mentoring, helping others grow or develop

Advance	Administer	Aid	Augment
Assist	Bestow	Donate	Endow
Facilitate	Foster	Give	Grant
Help	Impart	Improve	Invest
Minister to	Offer	Provide	Serve
Share	Strengthen	Support	Tithe

- **Create.** Inventing a product or service, writing articles or books, designing anything, such as being an architect or interior designer, composer, chef, jewelry maker, or fashion designer, floral designer, furniture maker, builder, craftsman, sculptor, artist, musician, screenplay writer, film director or producer, taking art, drawing, writing, or pottery classes

Assemble	Build	Birth	Craft
Create	Compose	Conceive	Concoct
Construct	Design	Develop	Devise
Dream	Evolve	Fabricate	Generate
Imagine	Ingenuity	Initiate	Innovate
Inspire	Invent	Make	Originate
Perfect	Plan	Start	Synthesize
Think			

- **Discover.** Work as a detective or investigator, learn new things, read books, take adult education courses or personal development courses, scientist, researcher, analyst, read nonfiction books to expand your knowledge

Absorb	Ascertain	Behold
Bring to light	Contemplate	Detect
Discern	Distinguish	Examine
Find	Gain	Investigate
Knowledge	Learn	Locate
Observe	Perceive	Penetrate
Read	Realize	Study
Spy	Uncover	Watch

■ **Feel.** Dance, do yoga, meditate, tai chi, learn to give Reiki or massage, take any experiential course or learn a profession such as healing, Reiki, or massage that will enable you to feel in your work, work in the intuitive or sensing fields, or sensory fields such as being a chef (taste), taster, perfumer

Awareness	Be with	Be in touch with
Dance	Emote	Experience
Feel good	Glow	Hear
Intuit	Notice sensations	Perceive
Sense	Scent	Taste
Touch	Vibrate	

■ **Lead.** Lead a team, company, or expedition, be a role model, take on leadership roles in the community or church, be a manager or boss, become a public speaker, be the leader of a cause or movement, be a leader in your field or hobby, influence or persuade others to your point of view

Be the chief	Cause	Direct	Dominate
Encourage	Enroll	Forge ahead	Govern
Guide	Head	Inspire	Influence
Lead	Manage	Model	Order
Persuade	Pioneer	Reign	Rule

■ **Master.** Become a master or expert in your field or hobby, take courses to refine and develop your natural strengths, reach the pinnacle of your vocation or craft, be a master woodworker, artisan, actor, singer, bond trader, teacher, doctor; continually strive to be the best, hone your skills, seek ongoing training, education, or coaching

Adept	Be the best	Champion
Conquer	Competence	Deft
Dexterous	Dominate field	Excel
Expert	Experience	Genius
Greatest	Know-how	Outdo
Preeminence	Primacy	Proficient
Prowess	Skill	Superiority
Superstar	Talent	Understanding
Wisdom		

■ **Play.** Have fun, go to the movies, shop, dance, paint, read for pleasure, eat in fine restaurants, have great sex, play games or sports, play card or board games, go to the theater or concerts, go to parties, entertain others, take a course for fun or pleasure, go to a comedy show, go camping, have a picnic, take a scenic drive

Amuse oneself	Be amused	Be sensual
Be entertained	Be hedonistic	Be merry
Caper	Comedy	Dance
Dining	Enjoyment	Frolic
Have fun	Joke	Laugh
Play games	Rollick	Revel
Sports	Sensuality	Sex

■ **Relate/Communicate.** Hold a family reunion, set up a family website to keep in contact, post photos, and chat online, join a group in your community, join or start a book club, have family dinners together, have friends and/ or family over for potluck suppers

Associate	Affiliate	Belong
Be part of a community	Be in touch	Be with family/friends
Bond	Connect	Communicate
Converse	Forge	Integrate
Involve	Link	Join
Speak	Talk	Unite

■ **Be Sensitive.** Become a healer, masseuse, therapist, counselor, or coach, visit children's, elderly, or disabled homes, volunteer or work for soup kitchens or charities, volunteer or work on a support phone line, volunteer to hold babies in hospitals

Be affected	Be present	Be compassionate
Be moved	Be tender	Care
Emote	Empathize	Feel
Melt	Perceive	Respond
Soften	Support	Sympathize
See	Take to heart	Touch one's heart

■ **Be Spiritual.** Join a church, religious, or spiritual group, meditate, journal, become a yoga teacher or do yoga, become a nun, monk, minister, or priest

Be aware	Be accepting	Be awake
Be passionate	Blessed	Canonized
Devout	Deify	Devoted
Glorify	Grace	Honor
Meditate	Piety	Practice holiness
Practice a religion or belief	Pray	Purify
Relate with God	Sacredness	Sanctify
Sainted	Theist	

- **Teach.** Become a teacher, trainer, lecturer, or public speaker, host a radio show, teach English in a foreign country, be an adjunct professor in your area of expertise at a local college or university, tutor children or adults, teach adult education classes, coach

Advise	Coach	Civilize
Consult	Cultivate	Demonstrate
Direct	Educate	Edify
Enlighten	Explain	Expound
Give lessons	Guide	Illuminate
Improve	Inform	Indoctrinate
Instruct	Lecture	Mentor
Preach	Prepare	Prime
Sermonize	School	Show
Train	Tutor	Uplift

- **Win.** Regularly engage in sports or games where you are likely to win, host a weekly card party, set goals and objectives so that you can win in your life, work with a coach or trainer to gain the edge over competition

Acquire	Accomplish	Attain
Attract	Be victorious	Be first
Conquer	Gain	Score
Triumph	Predominate	Prevail
Win over		

Now that you've circled your values, go back to your list of the best times in your life and see if you can match the values to the highlighted experience. Write down the corresponding value to each of the highlights of your life.

Sample Highlights/ Peak Experiences — **Core Value Expressed**

1. Living abroad in Spain — Travel/Adventure
2. Giving the high school speech — Lead/Inspire
3. Decorating home — Beauty
4. Going on a yoga retreat — Peace/Spiritual
5. Creating a new product — Create/Invent

My Highlights/Peak Experiences — **Core Value Expressed**

1. _____
2. _____
3. _____
4. _____
5. _____
6. _____
7. _____
8. _____
9. _____
10. _____

Do not worry if you have selected quite a few values. We love our values so pick ten or twelve of your favorites. Of these ten or twelve, write down the most important top four values (they may be a combination of being and doing values).

Top Four Core Values

1. _____

2. _____

3. _____

4. _____

Excellent! Now that you have your top four values in hand, you are ready to start designing your entire life around them. This is when life gets really fun and exciting and you'll start to effortlessly attract great people and opportunities.

8

. . . .

Orient Your Life
Around Your Values

THE SECOND BIG secret: *we are irresistible when we are doing what we love to do.* The best time to meet your soul mate is when you are living your top core values. You will be at your most attractive and, if your partner likes you when you are living your values, he or she will be more likely to encourage you to keep on living them. This makes for a very happy life together. So, whether you want to find your soul mate or you want to keep your soul mate, live your values. It will keep you attractive and exciting to your partner for a lifetime.

Now that you have identified your key values, it is time to start living them. I usually ask my clients to start by creating a values-based project or two, regardless of what else they are doing in their lives. For example, when I was working at the bank, I decided that in order to express my value to lead and inspire others, I could start by leading the First-Time Home Buyer's Seminar. I wouldn't have wanted to make a career out of this, but it was good practice for speaking in front of an audience. I also signed up for Toastmasters International on my lunch hour in order to develop my speaking skills. These were two actions I could take immediately to fulfill my values to lead and inspire. I also booked a holiday in Greece with my sister to satisfy my value of travel and adventure. It was a few years later when I was leading a coaching skills seminar in London that I met my husband (living both the travel and adventure value and leading and inspiring). So there you have it. Get out there and start living your values now, even if at first, it is on a small scale. Given the law of attraction that like attracts like, by starting small, you are getting the attraction process in motion and it will soon snowball into more of what you love.

A client was complaining about her boss and hated her job. I encouraged her to quit and start her own business oriented entirely around her values. Her values for creativity and expression led her into a copywriting and editing business that has since ballooned into an extremely profitable enterprise that enables her to travel and speak as well, something she had dreamed about doing. Once she stopped complaining about her work and started doing what she loved, she had the courage and confidence to break up with her boyfriend, realizing he was no longer the right man for her, and soon met and married a great guy. When we lack passion in one area of our life, it tends to suck the passion out of every other area. The way to break this vicious circle is to start adding the passion back in. Then the passionless areas are suddenly incredibly obvious and we work to change those as well. It doesn't matter where you start; just start, however seemingly small or insignificant the change.

Peak Experiences on a Regular Basis

· · · · · · · · ·

The key to ongoing happiness is to orient your entire life around your top core values. Ideally, you want to structure your entire life so that you are living your values all the time, every day. It may take a bit of time to do this (I had to quit my job and start my own business before I could fully express my values to lead and inspire people every day), but start with whatever you can do now. Do not wait any longer! Feel free to review your list of peak experiences in life and see if you can put some of those back into your life on a more regular basis. Take Suzanne, for example. One of her peak experiences in life was a yoga retreat she had taken eight years ago. I asked her to book in a quarterly weekend retreat for the rest of the year. Sure enough, she met a great man on one of the retreats and they started to date. Roy had a value for fun and loved playing squash. He decided to join the local sports center and found a squash partner that day. Gina had always dreamed of dancing so started taking classes at Fred Astaire and soon began entering dance competitions. This gave her so much joy that she had the confidence to leave her boyfriend of years and start dating other men. She met her husband on eharmony.com and they married four months later. I just heard from her and she is still dancing and absolutely thrilled with her husband.

Action Step

Things I can do right now, starting today, that express my core values:

Actions	Value Expressed
1. Play squash	Have fun/Sports
2. Scuba dive	Explore/Discover
3. Keep a journal	Create
4. Meditate	Balance/Spirituality
5. Volunteer at a charity	Contribute

When you are living your values, you are having a great time and don't feel the need of a relationship to provide joy and happiness for you. You are fully alive and complete. The attraction principle kicks in: when you don't *need* it, you are most likely to attract the relationship you *want*.

Don't Wait to Live Your Values

· · · · · · · · ·

Your values shape your future, and many of us defer living our values, and therefore our future, because we assume we need to wait for a partner before we can have these experiences. In truth, one of the best ways to attract the perfect partner into your life is to start doing all the things you've imagined you'd do with him or her in the future. For example, let's take a common one. Many singletons are renting an apartment thinking that when they get married, then they'll buy a home together. Here is the good news: you don't have to wait to be married to buy your own home. And fortunately, many people aren't waiting. The majority of shoppers at Home Depot (the home improvement store) are women, and they are rapidly filling up the how-to-fix-this-or-that classes as well. So, if you've been waiting, wait no more. Buy a house you can live in and enjoy now.

Perhaps you've been imagining you'd take skydiving lessons with your partner? Well, don't wait. Sign up for the next skydiving class and go by yourself. You might just meet your partner in the class, and even if you don't you'll be doing something you enjoy, which will give you joy and energy, making you more attractive.

What about travel? Have you been thinking about the places you'd like to go with your partner? Book your trip now to see those pyramids in Egypt or the Great Wall of China. If you are afraid to travel alone, see if you can go with a friend, but make a point of meeting new people on the road. Traveling alone is an excellent way to meet people. You are much more likely to strike up conversations with other travelers and be more open to meeting new people if you are alone. So muster up the courage and go for it solo.

Maybe you are waiting to get a puppy or pet until you meet the right partner. Go right out and find a puppy today. Everyone loves a puppy, so you'll meet plenty of people while walking your new pooch around the block.

Are you waiting to find the perfect career or job? Perhaps you are thinking that you have a good job and you should just hang on to it and then, when you have the security of a partner in a relationship to help with living expenses, you'll be able to afford to take some risks and experiment with going back to school for new training or start writing that novel. Don't wait! Get enrolled in evening classes that interest you now or start moonlighting with a sideline business.

Take a Course or Class That Leaves You Glowing

. . . .

Having regular sex or being in love can give you a nice glow, but if that isn't currently available to you, you can get that glow in other ways. Try taking a class that leaves you radiant. Try ballroom, swing, or salsa dancing. A good night on the dance floor would keep me glowing and excited about life for three days, so I'd go three times a week. People can tell just by looking at you whether you are lit up and enjoying life or are sitting at home in front of the TV. When I went to parties in New York, people I had never met would come up to me and say that I lit up the room. You too can stand out from a crowd. Just start doing something that makes you feel sexy and fabulous. Here are ideas from some of my clients:

- Horseback riding
- Racquetball
- Dancing (jazz, modern, ballet, swing—whatever you most enjoy)
- Mountain climbing
- Spinning classes at the gym
- Yoga
- Water, downhill, or cross-country skiing
- Soccer
- Hang gliding
- Pottery
- Painting
- Hiking
- Getting a massage
- Sitting in a Jacuzzi with a glass of wine

Now make your own list of activities that light you up, turn you on, and make you feel alive and wonderful.

1. _____
2. _____
3. _____
4. _____
5. _____
6. _____
7. _____
8. _____

9. _____

10. _____

Write down as many ideas as you can think of and pick one or two to get started with right away. Again, do this now. (I hope you are getting the message.)

Classrooms are a great place to meet new people. Moonlight and experiment with a new business idea in the evenings and weekends. Take a creative writing class and start working on that book or screenplay. If you think you don't have time now, just unplug the TV and hide it in the back of a closet. That usually frees up an instant twenty hours a week—enough time to take evening classes, start a hobby or small business, or moonlight in something that interests you.

Are you waiting to be the belle of the ball? Hankering for the big wedding? Why not host a formal ball or big party, charge an entrance fee (unless you can afford to treat everyone), and be Cinderella for the evening? One of my roommates was so keen to be a bride and have the big wedding that she married the first man who asked her. Unfortunately, he wasn't a very good choice and after the party was over, she was left with him. They divorced after a year. If you want to be the belle, do it now. OK, so skip the white dress, but you could have a very lovely ball gown. This doesn't preclude you from having a big wedding, but you might as well get the desire for a big, fancy party out of the way ahead of time. It will be good practice for planning your eventual wedding.

Make a list right now of all the things you've been waiting to do.

1. _____

2. _____

3. _____

4. _____

5. _____

6. _____

Good! Now pick one of them that is an expression of one of your top four values and start doing it now.

Are Your Values Compatible?

Once you've identified your own values, it makes sense to see whether they are compatible with your prospective partner's, since that is the "glue" for most successful marriages. You might like volunteering once a week in a local soup kitchen, but would you want to move to a developing country and help the locals on a full-time basis? You might enjoy babysitting for your partner's nephews on occasion but couldn't stand the thought of actually having children of your own. It is worth finding out if you have compatible life goals and values before you get seriously involved or worse yet, marry the person!

Test your compatibility by doing a value-based project together. For example, since I love travel and adventure, it makes sense for me to travel with a prospective mate before tying the knot, and this is just what we did. It turns out one of my husband's core values is "The Unknown" so traveling to places he has never been fulfills this value for him and I'm happy as well because it is a great adventure. Before we got married, we took a trip to Morocco and a road trip through Northern England. Nothing like a road trip to make or break your relationship! Every other time I've traveled with a man, it ended our relationship shortly thereafter, but not with my honey. We thoroughly enjoyed ourselves, and this brought us closer together as a couple. Although we don't have all four top values in common, we respect each other's values and have some key ones in common that we enjoy doing together. If you don't share core values with your partner, then you'll probably be heading in separate directions down the road.

My Top Four Values   **My Partner's Top Four Values**

1. _____   1. _____

2. _____   2. _____

3. _____   3. _____

4. _____   4. _____

Projects/Activities That Express Our Common Values

1. _____

2. _____

3. _____

4. _____

Identifying and living your values will make you feel turned on and excited about your life. The more excited you are about life, the more naturally radiant and attractive you will be. So don't wait! Start doing this good stuff immediately. If you love your life now, you'll be much more attractive to your future or current mate.

You are now ready for romance and some tips for being simply irresistible.

9
. . . .

Tips for Being
Simply Irresistible

CONGRATULATIONS! AT THIS point you have not only discovered what your top four personal and emotional needs are, but you have a system in place to automatically fulfill them. You have broken through any resistance that might have been holding you back and have asked your friends and family to meet your deepest needs so well that you have eliminated all vestiges of "neediness." You have firm and clear boundaries in place, which allows room for true intimacy to occur. Satisfied, confident, and content, you then went on to discover your top four values and have now been regularly doing what you love to do. You have restructured your life so that you are fully expressing your top core values on a daily basis. As a result, you naturally and effortlessly radiate joy and happiness. At this point you have probably already attracted numerous potential mates and now are wondering what to do with them all. This chapter has some simple tips that work for everyone to be irresistibly attractive. Chapter 10 walks you through finding that special someone without wasting any time.

The Nine Must-Know Tips

· · · · · · · ·

The following tips work for anyone, single or married, male or female, who would like to increase his or her overall attractiveness and become simply irresistible.

1. Let the World Come to You

Mary had a terrible crush on a particular fellow. Her heart just pitter-pattered every time she saw him. In an attempt to win his heart, she invited him to dinner one Friday night. Mary started planning a gourmet five-course menu—apricot brandy liver pâté, vichyssoise, chicken sautéed with shallots, cream, and white wine sauce served on a bed of rice with asparagus, followed by a green salad and then dessert of homemade heart-shaped shortbread cookies and lemon sorbet. She took the day off from work to cook. When he arrived with a bottle of wine, Mary made the mistake of telling him that she had taken the day off from work to prepare. This put undue pressure on the situation. They couldn't eat a fraction of the food. After dinner, they kissed a bit, but then he decided to leave. They saw each other perhaps two additional times, but Mary was the one trying to get close. He really wasn't at all interested. At the time, Mary was heartbroken.

Now Mary sees that she was throwing herself at him—how unattractive! If she was going to cook dinner, it should have been something incredibly simple and easy like meatloaf and mashed potatoes. She never should have taken the day off to cook. Mary was trying too hard to get him to like her, and that ruined any chance of having a relationship. She was putting too much pressure on too soon. When you are attractive, people come to you naturally and effortlessly. You don't have to seduce them or try to get them to like you or win them over. It takes work to seduce someone; attraction is natural and effortless.

2. Make Your Home a Sanctuary

Your environment has tremendous impact on your psyche. In fact, it has been said that your environment is a reflection of your mental state. Take a look around you. What does your environment say about you? How would a friend describe your home? Is it warm, cozy, and organized? Or is it cool, aloof, upbeat, or modern? Most important, how do you feel in your own home? Relaxed and peaceful? Is it easy to unwind in your home? Do you feel special, surrounded by things that you thoroughly enjoy? I have a set of bright chintz floral pillows that I absolutely love; just looking at them makes me happy. Surround yourself with luxurious items. Make sure that you love every single painting or piece of artwork that you have displayed. For objects that are too good to throw out that you don't love, put them in a cardboard box in your closet or better yet, give them to friends or charity. (Sometimes it is easier to get rid of stuff if you first store it and realize that you didn't miss it.)

The objective is to make your home not only clean and organized but also a reflection of who you are. The first place to start is your bedroom. Make this room a haven, a place to retreat and relax. If you have a TV in the bedroom, I'd recommend moving it out to another room; you'll sleep better.

Bob, a forty-seven-year-old, balding, and somewhat portly systems engineer, was worried that he would never find the woman of his dreams. He wanted to get married in the worst way. I put him to work fixing up his house and he tackled the project with gusto. He had always admired his sister's house because it felt good just hanging around there. I told him there was no reason why he couldn't create the same peaceful feeling in his own home. He started by getting rid of all the furniture he had never liked—a wobbly table, a worn sofa, a set of bookshelves. Then he repainted the house in bright colors that he loved—a deep blue in the living room and a racy red in the bedroom. Bob put in a new bathroom cabinet, replaced the old radiators, and put in new blinds. About halfway through this project, Bob met a dynamic and successful woman who just couldn't keep her hands off him. He was amazed. He kept working until he had the house just the way he wanted it. Now Bob's complaint was that she wanted more sex than he did. Definitely a new experience for him! While this relationship didn't last, it gave him a sense of confidence that he was attractive and could attract intelligent and exciting women. Set up your home so that it gives you energy. Take the time to make your home a sanctuary and it will restore and refresh you every day.

3. Keep a Gratitude List

One way to attract more of what you want in life is to be grateful for what you already have, even if it is not enough. We spend so much of our time and energy focusing on what we *don't* have that we often neglect to appreciate what we *do* have.

To remind yourself of all the wonderful things you have, at the end of each day take a few minutes to write down everything that you are grateful for. It could be your health or a beautiful sunrise or a cup of hot cocoa. No matter how rough a day, there is always something or someone to be grateful for—a partner to come home to who will listen to you, a dog that adores you, a warm bed to sleep in, or just that you survived that day with your limbs intact.

What is the attraction principle here? What you focus on expands. If you focus on what you don't have, you will attract even less. If you focus on what you do have, you will attract even more. If you are too needy or desperate, you will end up repelling the very thing you want to attract. When you are grateful for what you have, even when it is not enough, you'll attract more.

Here is a great end-of-the-year gratitude and wish ritual that you can do right now and then repeat on your birthday or at the end of the calendar year. First, make a list of all your accomplishments over the past year—the top fifty things that you accomplished or ways that you grew as a human being. The process of thinking back over the year will help you realize just how much you have done. Then on New Year's Day or on your birthday, light a candle and read aloud each of your accomplishments, taking the time to appreciate each one of them and be grateful. When you are grateful for what you already have, the universe will reward you with even more. What do you have to be grateful for?

Then write a wish list—a list of all the things you wished would happen or that you could have. Think fairy godmother sort of stuff that you have no idea how it can happen but want anyway. Most people find they end up attracting almost all of the things on the list by the end of the year without really thinking about it again. Make your gratitude list and then your wish list and tuck it away in a drawer. When you come back to look at in six months or a year, you'll be amazed at how much has come true.

4. Smile, Be Happy!

I used to live right in the middle of New York City. People don't smile as much there as they do in other parts of the country. Yet there is nothing so attractive as a smile. If you want to be irresistible, smile. It takes a lot more energy to frown and be grumpy than it does to be happy. Why waste your energy being unhappy when you can just decide to be happy? It really is a conscious choice. Thomas Leonard, the founder of Coach U, once said that while pain isn't optional, suffering is. Life has its ups and its downs and with that will inevitably come some pain. You can't avoid the pain, but you can choose whether or not to suffer about it. I always explain this by asking if my clients have ever seen a three-legged dog. When a dog loses a leg for whatever reason, he doesn't suffer about it. The pain is just as real, but he licks his wounds and gets on with life. Dogs don't wander about dejected and aimless because they are missing a leg. They are just as happy and excited to see you as before. Nor do they let this get in the way of finding a doggy mate. Life goes on with or without the leg. People are the ones who choose to suffer. This doesn't mean that painful things don't happen. It certainly doesn't mean that you won't ever cry or feel terribly sad. It is a joy to be sad when you are sad and it is a joy to be angry when you are angry. Revel in your feelings—enjoy them. Cry your eyes out if you feel like it. But overall, you are a happy camper because you've chosen to be happy.

You also have to ask yourself if you've set your life up to make yourself happy. I am always amazed at the number of people who are on medication for depression who are in jobs they hate. If you hate your job and are doing it eight or more hours a day, how can you expect to be happy? You aren't supposed to be happy. Your unhappiness indicates that you need to find a different job. Or for that matter, a different mate. If you aren't doing anything in your life that makes you happy, you probably will be depressed.

For a quick cure, make a list of all the things that make you happy and start doing those immediately. For example, one client takes a nightly bubble bath complete with candles, a glass of white wine, and a good book. This helped her relax and unwind after a stressful day of work. Another client decided to bike to work instead of drive and found this was a simple way to build in daily exercise and made him feel great at the start of every day. Another client is happiest when helping others so volunteers at a local hospital and visits both children and elderly. One woman loves babies but has no children of her own. She volunteers to hold babies at the hospital. Go eat an ice-cream cone in the park or take a kid to see the zoo. The more things you do that make you feel happy, the happier you'll feel. A bit obvious, yes, but it is amazing how often we don't take time to do anything at all that makes us happy. Unfortunately, watching TV doesn't make you happy, and that is what most do at the end of the day. Do something that will naturally put a smile on your face.

On the other hand, you can also fake it a bit. If you are not in the habit of smiling, it may take practice. Go smile at fifty people this week. Count them. Smile at the grocery store clerk. Smile at your boss. Smile at the parking lot guy. Smile at yourself. Every time you are in the bathroom, look in the mirror, give your best smile, and say, "Hi, good looking!" Even if you don't think it's true. In fact, especially if you don't think it's true. One client kept saying that he was ugly. He loved to dance but was often rejected by women on the dance floor at the local clubs. I asked him to do this exercise and one month later he told me women were asking *him* to dance! And if he asked a lady to dance and she turned him down, he would say, "That's too bad, you are missing out on a great turn around the floor." A scientific study proved that when you smile, the muscle movement releases endorphins in your body and you actually feel better. If you don't feel like it, fake it. Smile anyway for the practice and enjoy those endorphins. You'll look and feel irresistible.

5. Listen like You've Never Listened Before

Most people like to think that they are good listeners. Very few people actually are. Think about the people you know. Of all your friends and family, how many really listen to you? Listening is an art and, like any skill, takes practice. For most of us, no one ever taught us how to listen. We were taught to speak, but never to listen. *Listening is very attractive.* Stop worrying so much about what you are going to say and try keeping your stories to yourself.

Listening and keeping your stories to yourself will lead to an unexpected result. The person who does the most talking end up feeling like he or she knows and trusts the listener. It seems like it should be the reverse, that the person listening should feel like he or she knows the talker, but this isn't the case. A well-known reporter confirmed this. He said that the way to build trust in someone is to listen and keep on listening.

As a general rule, the ideal guideline would be to talk 20 percent of the time and listen 80 percent of the time. Try this today and see what happens. You might be surprised at the things people will tell you when you really listen. And they will love you for listening.

Here is a tip: if you are with someone and you aren't talking, but you are talking to yourself in your head, perhaps coming up with your response or judging and evaluating what the person is saying, you aren't really listening. You are talking to yourself in your head. Yes, *that* little voice that just said, "What are you talking about? I don't talk to myself." You might just as well get up and stand in a corner and talk to yourself. Next time you are listening to someone, notice how much you talk to yourself. Then shift your focus back to the other person. Hear everything he or she has to say before you even start to think of a response.

Listening is not so easy; it takes practice. Experiment. The more you listen, the more attractive you will be. And an excellent listener is simply irresistible.

6. Acknowledge People Profoundly

One simple and highly effective way to become irresistible is to convert your compliments into acknowledgments. People get compliments fairly often:"Oh, what a lovely sweater." Or,"You sure look handsome today!" Don't get me wrong, compliments are great, but acknowledgments are even better! An acknowledgment is about who the person is, while a compliment is usually about what the person has or does. For example, "Robert, I really appreciate the support you've shown by coming all the way out from New Jersey to attend this workshop. Your presence lights up the whole room." That's an acknowledgment; it is very personal and leaves Robert feeling great about himself. Think of some way you can acknowledge someone for who he or she is and be as specific as possible. Don't just say,"You're terrific." Say,"You're a skilful speaker. I admire how gracefully you handled that rude comment." Or,"You are a generous and loving person. You know just the right thing to say to make a person feel good." Instead of saying to the cook,"What a delicious dinner!" you could say,"This is a superb meal. Your attention to detail is incredible. Not only is this delicious but it is artistically and beautifully presented." People will want to be around you if you are in the habit of giving acknowledgments. You will also be energized because it feels really good to give acknowledgments. Just change this one little thing and you'll immediately be more attractive.

7. Be Sensuous

You have to slow down to become sensuous. Being sensual is not about sex, but about relishing your senses of sight, sound, taste, touch, and smell. Savor life and all its flavors and textures, its colors and shapes. We are physical beings in a physical world designed to be enjoyed and appreciated. In the rush of life it is easy to neglect the purely sensual side of our nature.

If you have lost touch with your sensuality, it is easily reawakened. After a bath or shower, rub a scented body oil all over. Do this slowly, massaging and enjoying the curves and lines of your body, the silky feel of your own skin and the oil. Instead of eating ice cream or sorbet with a spoon, order it in a cone. Enjoy the pleasure of licking it, twirling your tongue around the cold, sweet ice cream. Bake cinnamon rolls or put cinnamon sticks in boiling water on the stove to make the whole house smell delicious. Put beautiful artwork on your walls to give your eyes a visual feast. Drink champagne and toast the sunset. Wear clothes that are irresistible to touch—soft cashmere, silk, a fuzzy angora sweater, a buttery cotton, or a cozy flannel. Listen to music that you love. Try Pachebel's Canon or Ravel's Bolero. Chant the mantra "om" until you feel yourself vibrate with the sound. Read poetry out loud. Try an unusual dish with unfamiliar spices—an Indian curry, the hot chile spiciness of a Mexican dinner, or the searing burn of Thai food. You are a sensuous being. Revel in it!

Nature is full of its own sensuality: the soft curves of green hills, the vivid glow of a sunset, the methodic pounding of waves crashing on sand, the dreamy romance of a starry evening, the silken softness of a rose petal. If you've lost touch with nature, you've lost touch with some of your own natural sensuality. When is that last time you walked barefoot through the grass or sand? Make a point of spending at least a few hours a week surrounded by nature, even if that means having lunch in the park during the week. At the very least, buy some fresh flowers for your home and enjoy the beautiful fragrance and colors.

8. Be an Angel

Newsweek reported in a cover story that more than 60 percent of the population believes in angels. If you were an angel, what would you do for the people in your life? What secret favor could you do without anyone knowing you did it? Once you start doing angel acts, you will radiate and glow from the inside out. When you have your needs fully met you can afford to give without needing anything in return. If you have a hard time giving secretly, it is a sure sign that your needs aren't sufficiently met. Get your needs met first, then you'll be ready to give freely and easily. This is *not* about sacrifice or suffering. Don't do a favor for someone else if it will hurt you. You come first.

Here are some examples of angel acts: drop some cash off in an unmarked envelope for a friend or relative who is having a tough time financially. Send an anonymous donation to a charity of your choice. Throw change on the sidewalk in front of a school. Take out the trash when your spouse isn't looking. Send an anonymous note of appreciation to a friend. Stop by a home for the elderly and visit with people who look lonely. Rake the leaves in your neighbor's yard. Volunteer one day in a soup kitchen. Do a good deed or some random act of kindness.

Linda, a financial planner, was in a funk, feeling unloved and sorry for herself for no particular reason. I gave her the homework of giving love or some small gift to everyone she came in contact with. At work she said hello to the secretary and thanked her for always smiling no matter how she must feel. At the grocery store she let a person who just had two items go ahead of her in line. The person was grateful and appreciative and Linda felt oddly good for doing such a small favor. She smiled at the grocery store clerk and told him that he was doing a great job handling the eggs with care. As she was driving out of the parking lot, she waved another car ahead. By the end of the day, Linda felt completely fulfilled and thought that the world wasn't such a terrible place after all. She made it a great place simply by being an angel. Anyone can do this—yes, you too!

A client of mine house-sat for some friends in New York City for a weekend. As a thoughtful gesture, knowing my client had recently left his job to start his writing career, his friends had left him an envelope with some cash in it. Not a huge amount but a very nice gesture. They were wealthy and could afford to do this. But my client rejected this generous gift and felt too proud to accept it. What a shame! It is lovely when someone accepts a gift graciously. All you have to do is say, "Thank you!" After all, what right do you have to deprive someone of the joy of giving?

9. Develop Your Courage

One of the best ways to tackle fear is to start taking more risks in life. Consider these exercises to strengthen your risk muscle. I'm not suggesting that you do anything that would put yourself in physical danger, but rather that you start taking some little or even big risks. Why? Because taking a risk, doing something that might even scare you, will make you feel fully alive and vibrating. The fear will get your heart pumping and toes tingling. Plus, you'll become a stronger, more powerful human being. Here are some suggested risks to get you started:

- Ask your boss for a raise. Most people are underpaid for what they do, so ask!
- Call someone up you've been meaning to call and, for whatever reason, haven't.
- Ask someone to meet one of your needs.

- Apologize to somebody for something you did that hurt that person, even if he or she doesn't know you did it.
- Return something that you stole or "borrowed" with the appropriate apologies.
- Volunteer to give a presentation or speech.
- Take a trip by yourself.
- Take the opposing side of an argument. (Stand up for what you think.)
- Go to dinner by yourself at a nice restaurant.
- Take a class in scuba diving.

What is the relation to being irresistible? People who never take risks are rather dry and stale. They may be stuck in a comfortable groove that even they find boring by this time. A risk or two will freshen you up and shake loose any cobwebs that might have been gathering around you. What is something that you'd be afraid to do? Do it this week. Make a dare with your friends if you need to. Keep challenging yourself to do something new and scary and you'll attract wonderful opportunities.

Now that you are simply irresistible, it is time for a few tips on meeting that special someone. Read on.

10

. . . .

The Basic Rules of Dating: The Time Line

NOW THAT YOU'VE become irresistible and are attracting lots of potential mates, it's time to make sure you choose the right partner. Ladies, let's face it: if you want to have children, time is not on your side. I've personally experienced the inner sense of panic when you suddenly wonder if you might be too old to bear children and have no eligible man in sight, and I've also coached many high-powered executive women who were so busy in their careers that they missed the boat on having children altogether. So whether you want children or you simply don't want to waste time in a dead-end relationship, follow these simple guidelines.

Like Attracts Like

. . . .

Although the cliché is that opposites attract, it is much more frequent that *like attracts like*. If you want to attract a friend or special relationship into your life, one of the most effective ways to do this is to write down all the qualities that you'd like this person to have. Are they financially secure, generous, loving, adventurous, intelligent, self-confident, good-looking, athletic? Write down every single quality you can think of.

Now go back through your list and be even more specific. The reason it is important to be specific is that making a list is a very powerful exercise and you might find that the universe delivers up exactly what you put on the list. For example, one of the qualities one of my clients had written on her list was "intelligent" and likes to read books. Well, for years she went out with a very intelligent man who read books, never mind that those were computer manuals! When she reviewed her list, she realized that she was actually hoping to find someone who liked to read and discuss literature, so she made that item a bit more specific. Another woman had written the heading, "My Ideal Husband," above her list of characteristics and then wondered why she kept attracting married men (husbands).

Now that you have your detailed and specific list ready, go through and see which of those qualities you are missing in yourself—remember, like attracts like. Develop these qualities as soon as you can. When I was buried in credit card debt, I fantasized about meeting a Prince Charming who would be so in love with me that he wouldn't even blink at the debt and would wipe it clean for me. Of course, he would be fabulously wealthy. Instead I ended up attracting and dating a man who had money, but was incredibly tight and even insisted on going dutch. Hardly my idea of Prince Charming! But I had to learn how to get myself out of the financial mess I had gotten myself into. After I paid off my debts and had plenty of savings, it was easy to attract extremely successful and very generous men. Now that I didn't need their money, the men I dated always insisted on paying for dinner. So if you want to attract someone wealthy, the best way is to become wealthy yourself. If you want to attract someone who is adventurous, start having your own adventures today. Become the person you'd like to attract.

Weed Out the Unworthy

· · · · · · · ·

Refer to the list of characteristics that you're looking for in a partner. This is a good list to have on hand so that when you find someone, you can check through your list and make sure you aren't being blinded by love. Or conversely, you might not be terribly attracted at first and when you realize that he or she ticks off all your boxes, then you know it is definitely worth spending more time with the person to get to know him or her to find out if the attraction grows with time.

Now that you have your rather extensive list, go through it and highlight your top ten requirements. These are the things that your partner absolutely MUST have or it is a deal breaker for you. Some examples include: generous of spirit, wants to have children, shares my faith or religion, is financially stable and responsible, has honesty and integrity, loves his work but isn't a workaholic. Now make a list of the top ten things you can't tolerate that your mate must NOT have, for example, no smoking, no children, no drugs, no tattoos, not anal retentively neat, not stingy.

Neil Clark Warren, the founder of the online dating service eharmony.com, has conducted enough research in working with couples to say with certainty that if you marry someone with even one item on the Must Not Have list, you will very likely end up divorced, so there is no point in even going there. This is why it is important to have a clearly written list of your criteria in hand before you start dating because love can be incredibly blinding and you might find yourself saying, "Oh, but he or she is so perfect in every other way, I can overlook this one thing."

No one is perfect, but that doesn't mean you should accept even one of the top ten Must Not Haves. The moment you discover one Must Not Have, move on immediately. Do not try to change your partner. Don't kid yourself, you simply don't have the time. And, even if he or she promises to change, once married, your partner will probably revert to his or her normal style anyway. People are more hard-wired to be the way they are than we realize. Keep looking and you will find someone who will match your top tens.

A colleague called me one day to let me know that he was engaged, no doubt hoping for my blessings. I was a bit hard on him because I knew he was a passionate man and that his fiancée was not at all interested in sex. I asked him how he was going to handle this very real and important difference in desire. He assured me that they were seeing the two best sex therapists in the area and working on this issue at the time and were confident they would resolve it. They married and sure enough, it continued to be a problem. Within two years, she left him for another man and he was devastated. If it is this much work in the beginning, you have to be prepared that it isn't going to get better in the long run. If my colleague had listed sexual passion and desire as a Must Have, then he would have realized that no matter how many other boxes she ticked off, she wasn't going to fulfill this key requirement for him. Or conversely, if he had written on his Must Not Have list "sexual frigidity," that would have helped him see that this wasn't going to work regardless of how many therapists they saw. Make your long list of criteria, but stick to your top tens like glue. If you stick to them, you won't waste valuable time in a relationship that will inevitably go awry.

Now take time to think carefully and make your lists:

Top Ten MUST Haves:

1. _____

2. _____

3. _____

4. _____

5. _____

6. _____

7. _____

8. _____

9. _____

10. _____

Top Ten Must NOT Haves:

1. _____

2. _____

3. _____

4. _____

5. _____

6. _____

7. _____

8. _____

9. _____

10. _____

Expand Your Circle of Contact

· · · · · · · ·

Most people have a fairly limited circle of contact. If you add up all the names of your family, friends, and acquaintances, it will probably be about two hundred people. This is pretty much the average. So, if you want to meet someone who is "one in a million" you had better get busy. If you are in your late thirties, you may have a fairly firmly established regular crowd of friends that you hang around with. And, if you still haven't found your mate, then you need to do something to expand your contacts and get exposure to some different people.

John Gray mentions this in his now classic relationship book, *Men Are from Mars, Women Are from Venus*. While I certainly gained a few valuable insights from Gray, I have to admit I disagree with him on one point. He suggests doing things you don't like doing to find a mate. For example, go to a football game if you hate sports. And worse yet, if you are normally a late riser, get up early and walk the dog. I understand where he is coming from—he is encouraging you to expand your circle of contact. If you are a late sleeper and get up early to walk the dog you'll bump into that morning riser up at 6:00 A.M. every day—someone you normally would not meet if you are still buried under the covers. This looks like a great idea on the surface, but then, if you do end up getting married, you'll have to deal with the fact that your partner is bouncing out of bed and ready to start while you are just getting that second round of deep, lovely R.E.M. sleep. Not an insurmountable problem, but not ideal either. And, if you end up marrying the man you met at the football match, how can you complain when he is glued to the TV for every game of the season?

Why not do something you love or at least enjoy instead? Take up fly fishing, wine tasting, or golfing, or join a running club. You can try something new without trying something you don't like. This way, when you do meet the right mate, you are much more likely to stick together if you have at least one top core value in common.

Cast a Lot of Pebbles

· · · · · · · ·

If you want to be irresistible you need to allow people and things to come to you. Pushing, pressing, arm-bending, seducing, convincing, and persuading may work, but they are not, I repeat, *not* attractive. It is easy to waste an awful lot of time and energy trying to guide the ripples when you'd be better off casting more pebbles and seeing which ripples find their way back to you. If you are looking for a great relationship, it is easier and more fun to try a lot of different things. Travel to places you've always thought would be interesting or fun. Experiment with many different ideas and options and don't worry about it. Your job is to cast plenty of pebbles.

Go out with a lot of different people; don't get wrapped up with just one man or women who seems pretty good. We are all looking for that one in a million person, but how many people have you actually gone out with? Thirty? That's a long way from a million. You don't have to go out with a million people, but it would certainly improve your odds if you saw a few more people.

If you are trying to "win over" a particular person, let him or her go. It probably isn't worth it. Move on to the next and don't waste your time. Either it is fun and effortless to create a new relationship or it's not worth it. If you are working so hard to seduce someone, it probably won't work out in the end anyway, so you might as well cut your losses and find someone else. This is not to say that if you already have a good relationship, it doesn't take work to maintain it, but if you are struggling to make things work at the very start of a relationship, you can bet that the maintaining won't be a cakewalk.

The Two-Date Rule

· · · · · · · · ·

This may seem counterintuitive in a chapter about finding the right person as quickly as possible, but it's important not to rush from one relationship to the next to the extent that you miss out on some good opportunities. Give your dates a fair chance of two full dates if not three. The first date is the worst date in terms of assessing whether someone is going to be a suitable match for you. Most people are too nervous on a first date or are trying too hard to impress to relax enough to be themselves. For this reason alone you should always give your date at least one more chance. Sometimes our first impressions are quite right and sometimes they aren't. By the second date, you'll both be more relaxed and in a much better position to determine whether the person is worthy of seeing again or not. We've seen too many Hollywood movies and now expect to be bowled over with passion and excitement on the very first date. Sometimes this happens and love bursts like fireworks, but sometimes it is a long, slow burn.

One client, a forty-something, vivacious brunette, had a history of going out with really drop-dead gorgeous men. When she and her boyfriend walked down the street, people turned their heads to look at him, not her. Although this man was very attractive, he wasn't really her soul mate, and she knew it was time to end the relationship and start looking for her true love. She signed up for Internet dating and started perusing the eligible men. One fellow seemed very interesting but she almost deleted his profile because he wasn't particularly gorgeous. He looked rather average. He wasn't unattractive, but his hair was thinning a bit. I encouraged her to get past the looks and give the man a chance. They met and she discovered that, in person, he had real charisma and was much more attractive than his photo led one to believe. Yes, his hair wasn't much to speak of, but his eyes were a stunning brilliant blue and captivated her completely. She still wasn't sure, though, because she was convinced that she had to have a really good-looking man in order to feel sexually attracted to him. I urged to her to see him again, and sure enough, he started to grow on her. He was so thoughtful and considerate and charming, he became more attractive in her eyes and his real personality shined through. By the third date she wasn't even worried about his looks and was smitten. They continued going out and are now happily married. She thanks me for encouraging her to look beyond her mental pictures and give him a chance.

The Eight-Date Rule

To many, this tip will sound old-fashioned. It was advice my mother gave me when I started dating in high school (she doesn't even remember this, but I do!). Her sage wisdom was to wait to have sex until at least eight dates to ensure that the man you were with was worth the trouble and to make sure you weren't being swept away by the stars on a particularly romantic evening. Like it or not, it is the woman's job to hold back and give the relationship time to develop. Studies have proven that most men, if given the opportunity, will jump in the sack with just about anybody at just about any time.

I want to emphasize that this isn't about being manipulative or coy, but rather about giving a relationship enough time that you can assess whether the man or woman you are with fulfills your top ten requirements, and it also allows time for intimacy to develop. You simply can't rush intimacy. And, as a side benefit, in this world of instant gratification, it is refreshing to have to wait for something you want. It intensifies desire and makes gratification all that much more exciting and fulfilling. Don't deprive yourself or your partner of this lovely, heady anticipation.

You risk too much by having sex too soon. You could be rushing intimacy that your partner isn't quite ready for. You could be setting yourself up for heartbreak if you fall for this person and he or she hasn't fallen for you yet. You could be putting too many expectations on your partner for intimacy. For your own self-respect, it is a good policy to ensure that before you agree to have sex with someone, he or she is willing to be exclusive and not date other people. This will weed out those who are just looking for a good time or an easy conquest. There's nothing wrong with looking for a good time, mind you, but if you are looking for a committed relationship, then you don't want to waste time with those who are still playing the field. If they aren't ready or willing to commit to being exclusive, then under no circumstances should you sleep with them until they are. Dating is challenging enough without adding the complexities of sex to the equation. And men can't help but think that if you jump into bed right away with them, then you are doing the same with every other Tom, Dick, and Harry. You may have been waiting for "the one," but your partner won't believe you if you say that you don't usually act so quickly and were making a special exception for him.

Some women worry that they'll lose the man if they don't have sex fairly soon. They feel they have to have sex to create the bond and keep him interested. Wrong! If you lose a man because he won't wait eight dates, then you never had him in the first place.

The Six-Month Rule

· · · · · · · ·

This rule is especially for women wanting to have children. It is very easy to hang out in a comfortable, fun relationship with a good man for a number of years. Before you realize it, a few years can pass and while there may not be anything wrong with the relationship, it might not be right enough for marriage. Refer back to your list of criteria every six months and see whether a Must Not Have has appeared that you weren't aware of. Perhaps you've simply realized this isn't the one. After six months, you should have had enough time to get a fairly good grasp of whether you want to marry your mate or not. If you can't see future potential, then break up and start the dating process again.

On the other hand, if you think the relationship is growing and developing and has real potential, then you may want to give it more time. Mark your calendar six months forward and make a date with yourself to reassess at that time. You need to write it down because otherwise years could pass before you take stock. And you may not have the time to spare.

The Two-Year Rule

· · · · · · · ·

Again, this tip is especially for those women who want children. After two years, you certainly have had enough time to know whether or not this person is marriage material, and at this point, you need to either move toward future commitment such as engagement or move back to step one and start the dating process again. If you discuss getting married and your mate still isn't ready, then you need to break up and start fresh. Sometimes, you will find that this will shake up your partner enough to realize he or she doesn't want to risk losing you and will declare his or her intentions. Again, this isn't about rushing—after all, two years is plenty of time for both of you to get to know each other. However, two years is also a point of diminishing returns in that more time spent together isn't likely to reveal much more you haven't already learned. So it is time for a real commitment or time for you to realize your partner won't commit and you need to move on. Far better to learn that this person won't commit now than it is to wait another two years. By that time you could have recovered from your heartbreak and be happily ensconced with someone who doesn't have "commitment issues." When people say they aren't ready to commit, that typically means they think they might find someone "better" and are stalling for time. It might also mean your partner isn't sufficiently established in his or her career (especially with men) to feel like he or she can provide for a family. Or it could simply be that your mate thinks he or she should feel some overwhelming urge or desire to get married and doesn't because he or she is happy and perfectly comfortable with things just as they are. Most men don't have any big urge to get married and they don't have a biological clock that is ticking away creating a sense of urgency. For this reason, it makes sense to stick to the two-year rule.

Concluding Thoughts

You have now completed a very challenging and life-changing coaching program. You have identified and fulfilled your top four needs, you've expanded your boundaries and raised your personal standards, and you've found that you now effortlessly attract much better people and opportunities into your life. You've discovered what your core values or passions in life are and have restructured your life so that you are living and expressing these values on a daily basis. You love what you do and you love your life. You are irresistibly attractive and are in great shape to attract the love of your life effortlessly.

Is there a down side to being so irresistible? Yes, you might find that you need to upgrade your friends. There is often a bit of fallout. One client never realized that she was a chronic complainer until she started working on her life. Once she eliminated all the things she had been complaining about, got her unmet needs fulfilled and was no longer needy in any way, and started doing work she was passionate about, she stopped complaining. After all, there isn't much to complain about in a great life. She soon realized that her friends were still complaining and that their relationships had been based on mutual gripe sessions. You can gently inform your friends, "Let's do ten minutes of complaining and then move on to the things we are happy about." Or you might find that you upgrade your relationships in general. Do give people a chance, though, by using the four-step communication model you learned in Chapter 5. Remember, you were where they are not that long ago.

Other people find that they are suddenly attracting a lot of really great people and opportunities, and sometimes that gets a bit scary or even overwhelming. Our own natural power is often more than we realize, and that can be daunting. You will very quickly need to learn to say no to what you don't want. One forty-two-year-old singleton never expected to attract more than 150 matches on eharmony.com and was worried about how she would find the time to respond to them all. (I told her to ruthlessly weed them out.) One of them she is very excited about, as he ticks off all the right top tens on her list. You'll tend to attract people who are just a step ahead or a step behind you, so if you've attracted them, then good for you! You can trust that the law of attraction really works and in the vast majority of cases, like really does attract like. It isn't a mistake. If you don't believe you deserve it, you might sabotage the opportunity. Get over the notion that you need to deserve something to have it. Trust that if you have attracted a great person or a fabulous opportunity, then that is because you are great and fabulous too! And, everything happens when you are ready, so even if you don't *feel* like you are ready, if you attracted it, you are.

Finally, it is never too late. A client in her early forties found her husband while traveling for two weeks in Italy and brought him back to Manhattan. Another client had healthy twin girls at the age of fifty-five (although I don't advocate waiting that long if you can help it). And I didn't meet my husband until I was thirty-seven and was giving a seminar in London. I had my first girl at thirty-nine and the second at forty-one. So get out there and enjoy your newfound powers of attraction!

APPENDIX

· · · · · · · ·

How to Find or Become a Coach

Finding a Coach

· · · · · · · ·

HERE WE ARE at the end of the book and at this point, you probably see a few areas in your life that need some work. It doesn't take forever to attract the success and the life you want. The rewards are well worth the work and start to kick in immediately, so don't wait—start today. If you want to make it easy on yourself, hire a coach to help you through this process and keep you on track. Left to our own devices, we don't progress as quickly. We all have blind spots and it is helpful to have an outsider point them out. Anyone who has hired a personal trainer knows it is much more fun to go to the gym or do ten pushups with someone egging you on and keeping an eye on your posture than trying to do it alone. The same goes for a life coach. When you are discouraged and ready to quit, you can count on your coach to be there to keep you going through the tough spots. You can count on your coach to tell you the truth.

Your friends and family can't always tell you the truth because they don't want to risk the relationship or because they have their own agenda in mind.

Here are some pointers on finding an excellent coach.

- Hire a professional, someone who has been through a specialized coach-training program so you know he or she has some basic skills. Plenty of people are suddenly calling themselves coaches when in fact they are therapists, counselors, or consultants and have never completed a real coach-training program.

- When you interview the coach, you should feel that you can tell this person the whole truth; is this a person you can confide in? A person you trust and respect? Do you feel listened to and understood?

- As a general rule, do not hire a close friend or a family member, for the reasons mentioned above. You don't want the coaching to affect your relationship. You can always fire your coach, but you can't fire your cousin or uncle. Keep friends and family for love, support, and encouragement.

- Does this coach have the experience, skills, and qualifications you are looking for? Don't be afraid to ask to speak to some of the coach's clients for a recommendation, especially those who had success in the area you want to develop. Ask what is the coach's style and philosophy and whether he or she has any specialties. Some coaches specialize in relationships, some in working with creative clients, some with entrepreneurs, people with head injuries, you name it. Whatever your particular need, you can guarantee that there is a coach out there who specializes in it.

- Don't worry about where the coach lives. Most coaches work by telephone, as it is more effective and efficient than in-person meetings. My clients are all over the globe and most of them I've never met in person. It makes no difference to the results they achieve.

- If you aren't having fun and seeing results with your coach, tell your coach what you need from him or her. If that doesn't work, ask for a referral to a different coach. In the first few sessions of coaching you will typically assess your current situation and talk about where you'd like to be. In a corporate setting you may discuss how the company goals work in relation to your own. You can expect your coach to provide ongoing positive support and encouragement, to ask you to go beyond where you'd normally stop, to press you to try new skills, to provide follow-up discussion on the goals you are working on, and to give you life work assignments every week. It is also perfectly OK to tell your coach how you are best coached. I usually ask my clients this anyway.

Whenever you find yourself getting bogged down or overwhelmed with a project, it is a good idea to find some help, whether that is a tutor to help you decipher a new computer program, a professional organizer to get your home in order, or a coach to help you live your dreams and attract everything you've always wanted. You can do this!

International Coach Federation

2365 Harrodsburg Road, Suite A325
Lexington, KY 40504
(888) 423-3131
Toll-free: +1-859-219-3580
Fax: +1-859-226-4411
E-mail: icfheadquarters@coachfederation.org
coachfederation.org

The ICF is an organization of professional coaches that hosts an annual coaching conference in addition to providing an extensive referral list of coaches and a Web-based referral service to help you find the right coach. They also offer three levels of coaching certification: ACC (Associate Certified Coach), PCC (Professional Certified Coach) and the highest designation, MCC (Master Certified Coach).

Lifecoach.com

(407) 628-2909
E-mail: faye@lifecoach.com
lifecoach.com
All coaches listed on this international coach referral service are graduates or in training at an ICF-accredited training program. Try a free half-hour coaching call with any that are available.

Talane Coaching Company

Talane Coaching Company provides you with the latest in coaching technology and the most highly trained coaches in the world. Your coach will help you design the life you have always wanted. The company offers the following services:

- Individual coaching
- Group coaching
- Corporate coaching
- Keynotes and workshops
- Retreats and seminars designed to meet the needs of your organization or group
- Monthly phone classes via an internationally accessible teleconference call

For a free e-mail subscription to *Talane's Tip of the Week* and/or her quarterly newsletter, send an e-mail to subscribe@ talane.com or sign up directly at the website: talane.com

To take the Emotional Index Quiz online, please go to emotionalindex.com.

For a list of upcoming phone classes, please go directly to talane.com or contact our company at the address below.

For more information on any of these services, please call, write, or e-mail:

Talane Coaching Company
Attn: Faye Morgan
4017 Corrine Drive
Orlando, FL 32814
(407) 628-2909
(888) 4-TALANE
E-mail: info@talane.com
talane.com

Becoming a Coach

For a complete listing of all the accredited coach training schools and organizations, please see the International Coach Federation website at coachfederation.org.

Programs vary widely in quality and content.

CoachInc.com
admissions@coachinc.com
1-800-48COACH

Attend the free CoachInc.com Question and Answer TeleClass to learn about the programs and services offered by Coach U and Corporate Coach U. Also available is "Becoming a Coach," a four-week course conducted via highly interactive TeleClasses.

This course shares valuable information about beginning your own coaching practice and allows you to hear and experience coaching. The Core Essentials program, where everyone begins training, is both challenging and fun and takes approximately fifteen months to complete. New coaches are also encouraged to participate in the Mentor Coach program to find an experienced mentor coach.

The Coaches Training Institute
4000 Civic Center Drive, Suite 500
San Rafael, CA 94903
(415) 451-6000
(800) 691-6008
thecoaches.com

If you would like an admissions advisor to contact you, please use the Contact Us form on the website and someone will respond within one business day. For general information, write to CTIinfo@thecoaches.com

RESOURCES

· · · · · · · · ·

Books

· · · · · · · ·

Csikszentmihalyi, Mihaly. *Flow: The Psychology of Optimal Experience.* New York: Harper Perennial, 1990.
■ A fascinating study on the state of consciousness called flow—a state of concentration so focused that it amounts to absolute absorption in an activity.

Fromm, Erich. *The Art of Loving.* New York: HarperCollins, 1956.
■ Learning to love, like any other art, demands practice and concentration, insight and understanding. The psychoanalyst Erich Fromm discusses all aspects of love from romantic to brotherly, self-love to spiritual love.

Glassman, Bernard, and Rick Fields. *Instructions to the Cook: A Zen Master's Lessons in Living a Life That Matters.* New York: Bell Tower, 1997.
■ If you lack the motivation to start work on your own special project, this little book will inspire you. You will learn to use what you have and recognize your faults as your best ingredients.

Jones, Laurie Beth. *The Path: Creating Your Mission Statement for Work and for Life.* New York: Hyperion, 1996.
■ Step-by-step process for creating a mission statement for your life that can be used to initiate, evaluate, and refine all of life's activities. Excellent questions to answer to create your own life plan.

Leonard, Thomas J. *The Portable Coach: 28 Surefire Strategies for Business and Personal Success.* New York: Scribner, 1998.
■ Leonard, the founder of Coach U, has packed most of the coaching curriculum into this book. It contains excellent checklists—the same ones that coaches use with their clients. A very good resource book for anyone interested in coaching.

Maslow, Abraham H. *Toward a Psychology of Being.* 2nd ed. New York: D. Van Nostrand Company, 1968.
■ The original academic source for the hierarchy of needs and the concept that emotional needs are requirements for our well-being and self-actualization comes from Maslow. Read this to understand his early work on needs and their critical role in the process of human growth, development, and self-actualization.

Miedaner, Talane. *Coach Yourself to Success: 101 Tips from a Personal Coach for Reaching Your Goals at Life and in Work.* New York: McGraw-Hill, 2000.
■ If you haven't already read my first book, it is full of simple yet powerful coaching tips to make you more successful in all areas of life. If you are struggling to meet your needs, you might want to start with this book and then move on to *The Secret Laws of Attraction.*

Pert, Candace B. *Molecules of Emotion: Why You Feel the Way You Feel*. New York: Scribner, 1997.
■ A fascinating and scientific account by the neuroscientist who made the groundbreaking discovery of how emotions and health are linked at a molecular level.

Richardson, Cheryl. *Take Time for Your Life: A Personal Coach's Seven-Step Program for Creating the Life You Want*. New York: Broadway Books, 1998.
■ Richardson is one of my coaching colleagues and she outlines an excellent program for extreme self-care.

Tieger, Paul D., and Barbara Barron-Tieger. *Do What You Are: Discover the Perfect Career for You Through the Secrets of Personality Type*. Boston: Little Brown and Company, 1992.
■ This book uses the Myers-Briggs Type Indicator (MBTI) to help you identify your personality type and your natural strengths and then suggests possible careers that match. This will help you strengthen your strengths and give up struggling.

Smith, Manuel J. *When I Say No, I Feel Guilty*. New York: Bantam Books, 1975.
■ If you say yes more often than you should, read this classic for some straightforward guidelines to end the doormat syndrome once and for all.

Tucker, Nita, with Randi Moret. *How Not to Stay Single: 10 Steps to a Great Relationship*. New York: Crown Trade Paperbacks, 1996.
■ If you are serious about finding the right partner I'd highly recommend this excellent program. I have coached several clients through the ten steps outlined and it works.

Warren, Neil Clark. *Date . . . or Soul Mate?: How to Know if Someone Is Worth Pursuing in Two Dates or Less.* Nashville: Thomas Nelson, Inc., 2002.

■ A quick read written by the founder of the terrific online dating service eharmony.com that will help you sort out what characteristics and qualities are most important and essential to you in a relationship.

Professional Organizers

· · · · · · · ·

National Association of Professional Organizers
4700 W Lake Avenue
Glenview, IL 60025
(847) 375-4746
napo.net

If you are struggling to get organized, call this association for a referral to a professional organizer in your area. They offer an e-mail referral service too.

Assist U
Contact: Stacy Brice
Toll-free: (866) 829-6757
assistu.com

For a referral to a well-trained virtual assistant who will handle administrative, accounting, and other tasks, contact Assist U. This company also trains people to become virtual assistants.

Help Children

· · · · · · · · ·

Big Brothers Big Sisters
230 North Thirteenth Street
Philadelphia, PA 19107
(215) 567-7000
Fax: (215) 567-0394
Bbbs.org

Big Brothers Big Sisters has been providing one-on-one mentoring between adult volunteers and children at risk since 1904. If you feel like you don't have enough love in your life and you like children, this might be just the place for you.

Allow The Children
Contact: Sue Cook
1969 Bethel Church Road
Forest, Virginia 24551
(434) 525-8866
allowthechildren.org

You can sponsor a child with this Christian organization. Your donations go directly to helping the children in poverty-stricken areas of the world such as Nepal and Burundi.

Help Yourself

· · · · · · · · ·

1-800 Flowers
1800flowers.com

Send gifts, flowers, or potted plants to someone or order them for yourself.

American Massage Therapy Association (AMTA)

500 Davis Street, Suite 900
Evanston, IL 60201
(847) 864-0123
Toll-free: 1-877-905-2700
Fax: (847) 864-1178
E-mail: info@amtamassage.org
amtamassage.com

Search online or call for a referral to a licensed massage therapist in your area.

Associated Bodywork and Massage Professionals (ABMP)

28677 Buffalo Park Road
Evergreen, CO 80439
(800) 458-2267
abmp.com

Call for referrals to massage therapists as well as other types of bodywork professionals.

Association of Image Consultants International

(800) 383-8831

Call this number for referrals to a professional image consultants in your area. I recommend that you interview a few consultants before making your final choice.

Associated Skin Care Professionals

1271 Sugarbush Drive
Evergreen, CO 80439
(800) 789-0411

Call the ASCP for a skin care professional in your area.

INDEX

· · · · · · · · ·

ABOUT THE AUTHOR

· · · · · · · ·

ONE OF THE most widely recognized coaches in the world, Talane Miedaner, author of the international bestseller *Coach Yourself to Success* and owner and founder of Lifecoach.com, has gained international prominence as a life coach by guiding thousands of people to wealth, success, and happiness. As a leader in the cutting-edge field of personal and professional coaching, Talane helps people structure their lives so that they can easily attract the opportunities they want in life. Her team of coaches works with executives, managers, public officials, entrepreneurs, corporations, and business owners around the world in person, by phone, and online. Talane leads numerous seminars and workshops nationally and internationally, and occasionally teaches at Coach U where she received certification as a professional coach. She is a member of the International Coach Federation and a Master Certified Coach. She has also published the dynamic audio program, *Irresistible Attraction: A Way of Life*, as well as a workbook for coaching.

Talane holds a degree in international affairs from the School of Foreign Service and a master's in English from Georgetown University. Prior to becoming a coach, Talane held a corporate position as second vice president at Chase Manhattan Bank.